The Two Deaths
of George Wallace

The
Two Deaths
of
George Wallace

The Question of Forgiveness

THOMAS S. HEALEY

Black Belt Press
Montgomery

Black Belt Press
P.O. Box 551
Montgomery, AL 36101

Copyright © 1996 by Thomas S. Healey. All rights reserved under International and Pan-American Copyright Conventions. Published in the United States by the Black Belt Press, a division of the Black Belt Communications Group, Inc., Montgomery, Alabama.

Library of Congress Cataloguing-in-Publication Data
Healey, Thomas S., 1930–
    The two deaths of George Wallace : the question of forgiveness / Thomas S. Healey.
        p.   cm.
    Includes bibliographical references.
    ISBN 1-881320-65-0 (alk. paper)
    1.Wallace, George C. (George Corley), 1919- –Assassination attempt, 1972. 2. Bremer, Arthur H., 1950- . I. Title.
F330.3.W3H43   1996
973.924'092–dc20
[B]   95-49435
                                                         CIP

Design by Randall Williams
Printed in the United States of America

        96 97 98   4 3 2 1

The Black Belt, defined by its dark, rich soil, stretches across central Alabama. It was the heart of the cotton belt. It was and is a place of great beauty, of extreme wealth and grinding poverty, of pain and joy. Here we take our stand, listening to the past, looking to the future.

For Mia

Marilyn Elizabeth Walters Healey

For whom the first poem was Writ

Contents

Making our history into literature becomes a way of confessing the limits of our knowledge, of expressing our hope to find some meaning in experience, and of playing on the frontiers.

DANIEL J. BOORSTIN

Acknowledgments

No writer works completely alone. Behind him are any number of people offering suggestions, criticism, help, encouragement, and, on occasion, condolences. All of these flowed freely from my friend and agent, June Cunniff, of the public relations firm J. Cunniff and Associates in Birmingham, Alabama.

There was one other person who had to be satisfied with this book. Mia Healey performs the invaluable task of reading everything I write with a fresh eye, refined taste, and elevated intelligence. If anything is unclear, or in conflict with something else, or simply hits a wrong note, she will unfailingly find it and march it in to me for correction. Meeting her rigorous standards for total quality is not always easy, but it does render a great sense of accomplishment.

I am indebted beyond words to those friends who took time to read the manuscript and offer comments, or to extend support in other important ways: Anstice Carroll, Lillian Craigie, Ruth Davies, Marjorie Downey, Virginia Schmedes, Helen Kromer Sharpe, and Lee van Laer. I am most grateful also to Betty and Henry Brown and Louise and

Doctor William Welch for their work with me over the years in exploring many of the ideas presented in this book. And finally, my gratitude to my brother, Bill Healey, who, without knowing how, helped to clarify the basic theme.

To all of these people, my heartfelt thanks. They have, in one way or another, contributed to whatever is of value in this work. I alone am responsible for its shortcomings.

Introduction

This book originated in a small Alabama town in 1962. I was one of a handful of corporate representatives on hand to announce that a tire plant would be built on a nearby site. We greeted local officials, met the press, and dutifully said nothing about the white and black drinking fountains and segregated stores. It bothered us, but our mission was to charm the people, not try to reform them. We had invited Governor John Patterson to attend, but Patterson's term was almost over so he sent a representative to say a few words in his stead. The representative he chose was the Democratic gubernatorial nominee, also known as the Governor-elect in those one-party, Solid South days.

The Governor-elect was George Wallace, a political unknown outside his state at the time. Typically, he could not confine himself to just a few words. He heaped praise on the company, promised to help smooth over any difficulties for us once he took office, expounded on his intention to make Alabama the most attractive state for new business, and invited us all to call him if we had any problems or questions whatsoever.

Later, at a luncheon in the local country club, I gazed in wonder at Wallace's energy and intensity. He never relaxed for a moment. Not only did he dominate the table with the force of his personality, cowing a delegation of ego-rich New York executives into silence, he actually extemporized a speech. Sitting on the edge of his chair and jabbing the air with his forefinger, he let us in on the future as he saw it. If those politicians in Washington send marshals to integrate Alabama's schools, he boomed, we'll meet 'em at the border with the state police. We know how to handle our "nigras" here. We know what works and what doesn't. Those agitators up North don't know anything about the folks here. The people of this state will never tolerate. . . . And so on and on.

All the while, I watched the black waiters slipping food in front of Wallace and the rest of us, wondering if they had slipped anything extra into the food. They displayed the most perfect poker faces I have ever seen, the faces of people making themselves invisible. Over the years, I have speculated whether the wearers of those unreadable expressions were, like many blacks of that time, spending their evenings helping plan the resistance to segregation that later led to the Birmingham riots and awakened the conscience of white Americans.

In any event, Wallace practiced his speaking skills on us. We could see that he was just staying warm for the next audience. This man was obviously going to make himself known. It seemed an interesting, if overreaching, ambition. After all, how could a mere governor of Alabama ever become a national figure?

Twenty-six years and several lifetimes later, I was back in Alabama as an independent writer. I had met June Cunniff, a highly accomplished Birmingham public relations executive, and agreed to try my hand on a book about George Wallace for an editor she knew. I was intrigued that so little attention had been paid to Arthur Bremer, the man who shot Wallace. What were all the forces, all the twists and turns, all the lines that had to cross to bring the famous politician and the unknown gunman together in a storm of bullets that changed the nation's contemporary history?

In Birmingham, June provided me with a base of operations at her offices while I made contacts and pursued the elusive Cornelia Wallace— Wallace's second wife—for an interview. Wallace's palace guard kept me away from him.

Cornelia is an interesting woman, the archetypal Southern steel magnolia—full of lightweight chat delivered in a musical voice as she made iced tea and fussed about my comfort. But when we settled in to talk and I switched on my tape recorder, she changed in front of my eyes. The magnolia was gone; I was in front of steel. As I referred to the questions I had written down in advance, she waved her hand impatiently. As niece of former Governor Big Jim Folsom, she had spent part of her childhood living in the Governor's Mansion, knew Alabama politics and politicians, and did not welcome time-wasting questions that could be answered else-where. I could see that this strong-willed woman would have risked her life to protect her husband, as she did when she flung herself onto a fallen George Wallace at the Laurel Oaks shopping cen-ter.

The next couple of hours put me through a crash course in Alabama history, Alabama psychology, Alabama religion, Alabama politics, government in general, and the overall wisdom and folly of the human species. She told me a number of things about Wallace that I could not verify and so could not use. Nor was I especially interested in doing so. My own agenda for this book was already taking shape.

It was night when Cornelia walked me out to my car. We stood there a while, trading confidences about the unforeseen vagaries of our lives. I have not seen Cornelia since, but her effect was to give this work a dimension it would otherwise have lacked.

Out of office for years, old, deaf, in constant pain, frequently needing emergency care for illnesses re-lated to the shooting, George Wallace nevertheless continues to exert a remarkable hold on our imagi-nation. His staying power in the public conscious-ness has never flagged. You can love or hate George Wallace, forgive or condemn him, admire or revile him. But you can never ignore him. His fingerprints are all over American politics. His former segrega-tionist views aside, Wallace saw many issues more clearly than his contemporaries did. He stood loudly against what he viewed as a bloated, over-regulating, over-taxing, intrusive federal government. That government provided his favorite targets: the coddling of criminals, the abuses of the welfare state, debased standards of behavior, the growing burden of taxes on those who could afford it least, and the arrogance of elected officials and their advisors toward the voters who put them in office. As a new century approaches, these themes continue to reverberate throughout—indeed, to bedevil—the nation's public life.

This book obviously is not intended to be a definitive biography of the man still known in Alabama as "the Guvnor." It has an entirely different purpose, which I hope will be clear to the reader as it unfolds.

I

Sending Messages

NATURE DESIGNED GEORGE WALLACE'S BODY, brain, and gut for politics.

The body was compact, powerful and enduring—a fighter's body, able to take punishment and give it. It was made for the rigors of campaigning from the dirt-poor backwaters of rural Alabama to the rusted grandeur of Northern cities. That physical endurance would keep George Wallace alive for years as a paraplegic with his spinal cord permanently damaged by an assassin's bullet.

The brain cells devoted to memory had an elastic quality. They were able to store a phenomenal amount of information, especially names and faces. Wallace could meet someone, exchange pleasantries, and years later run across the same person and ask after his wife Luella, and did his scalawag son Jimmy Joe recover all right from the arm he broke playing junior high school football.

And politics was in his belly, right in the center of his emotions. Even on the rare vacations he allowed himself with his beautiful wife, Cornelia, Wallace would restlessly thumb through books on history and politics, while she enlightened herself with the novels of Jacqueline Susann.[1]

Politics was George Wallace's vocation—he was, after all, a career governor of Alabama for a record four terms—his avocation, his passion, the real wife of his bosom.

And from his birth on August 25, 1919, politics was his road to power, money, and prestige, as it was for many bright but poor white men in the Alabama of his day.

Even as a small boy in Clio, a town of nine hundred souls in central Alabama's Black Belt—so named because of the color of its rich soil—Wallace showed a keen interest in adult matters and liked to spend his time talking with grown-ups. Both his father and grandfather held elective office, so Wallace came naturally to the fascinations of politics.

Wallace's own run for power began at the age of thirteen, when he campaigned locally for Fred Gibson for Alabama secretary of state. Gibson lost but Wallace found his passion. At sixteen, he became a state Senate page. He was elected to a number of student offices while pursuing a law degree at the University of Alabama in Tuscaloosa, supporting himself driving a cab and washing dishes. Although his family wasn't poor, he had so little money that he had to borrow textbooks from friends. But that was all right. With his remarkable memory, he didn't have to keep them very long. He displayed a special talent for constitutional law, which undergirded not only his political ambitions but also his later confrontations over state's rights with the Kennedys and other federal officials.

Like many short men, George Wallace was aggressive. As a boxer in high school, he pummeled enough opponents to win the Golden Gloves bantamweight championship of Alabama in 1936, and again the following year. His accomplishments in the ring, added to his judicial feistiness, later earned him the sobriquet of "the fighting little judge." He stood five feet seven inches tall and never weighed more than one hundred fifty pounds.

As an Air Force flight engineer during World War II, Wallace had to fight a pair of much more serious opponents. The first was spinal meningitis, which he contracted during training. He spent six days in a coma, coming as close to death as he would for many years. The illness cost him some of his hearing.

While recuperating, he married his first wife, Lurleen Burns, a department store clerk. In 1966, legally unable to succeed himself after his first term as governor, Wallace ran her as a stand-in governor, holding the office for him until he could regain it. Lurleen did her duty in this regard but also exceeded everybody's expectations. A warm and intelligent woman, she worked hard to improve conditions for women in the state's mental hospitals and at times defied Wallace's wishes about legislation. She won the hearts of Alabamians and became a popular governor before dying of cancer in 1968, leaving Wallace with four children. Three years later, Wallace married Cornelia Ellis Snively.

In Jacqueline Kennedy's heyday, Cornelia quickly became known as the most beautiful woman in American politics.

Always attractive—and attracted—to women, Wallace never suffered the constrictions of matrimony. "He had women," declared Cornelia. "George was a passionate man."[2]

Wallace received partial disability for his second opponent, nervous disorders that resulted from flying bomber combat missions as a flight engineer in the South Pacific. He recovered with psychiatric help. Later on, when his political enemies reminded voters that Wallace had needed the services of a shrink, he countered that at least he had been officially certified as sane, which was more than his opponents could claim. Point well taken: The issue soon died of neglect.

Home from the war, he set out on his long political career. That trail led through the assistant state attorney general's office, the state legislature, the 1948 Democratic convention as an alternate delegate, circuit judge for three counties, and his first, unsuccessful, run for governor. Wallace had grown up as a racial moderate and he ran on other issues. But Alabama at the time was the breadbasket of segregation. He was defeated soundly by segregationist Attorney General John Patterson. "Boys," legend has Wallace saying to his inner circle on the night of the loss, "I'll never be out-niggered again."[3]

And in the 1962 gubernatorial campaign, he wasn't. He played the race card brilliantly. And so, on January 14, 1963, at the age of forty-three, George

Corley Wallace was sworn in as Alabama's forty-ninth governor, thundering his most memorable line, "Segregation now, segregation tomorrow, segregation forever!"

Wallace finally had power that counted. Power to control events, power to *be* something.

Not everybody possesses the necessary qualities of personality to orchestrate the feelings and behavior of people on a mass scale. Wallace did. He was a master. Whether viscerally or intellectually, he understood the primacy of emotion over thought. He grasped the essential fact that emotion is energy. Emotion animates while thought temporizes and rationalizes. And Wallace, genuinely passionate about the average working man and woman, had the rare ability to reach out and shake a mass audience into action. He rode his followers' emotions like a cowboy on a wild bull, deftly controlling the action while the bleachers shook with bellows of approval.

That's real power, the power of personality, and it was to keep George Wallace in the public eye long after he outlived the power of office.

So by 1972, George Wallace had a dream of national power, and it was gaining substance as well as form. Make way, folks, here came a man who could shape the entire Democratic party's politics and principles. Why, he might even broker its presidential nominee later in the summer. That would put the pugnacious little governor—with the brown, slicked-back hair that always appeared jet-black in photographs, the flashing eyes and bulldog face—

right up there alongside the giants of the national political scene.

At that very same time, Arthur Herman Bremer had his own dream of power, but it kept receding the more he grasped for it. His dream was of the power of personality. To be looked at with admiration, even awe, instead of ridicule. To be loved. To count for something in this shitty world that kept edging away from him, that toyed with him and laughed and laughed as he ran this way and that, banging his head against his own meaninglessness.

But he could change all that in an instant. With careful planning, with willpower, with persistence, with a little luck, and with one of his concealed handguns, he could announce himself to history. Here I am, world! Hey, hey, how about *me*? Now who's the real mover and shaker? Now who has the last hard laugh?

On a spring day in 1972, the two dreams collided in the same space at the same time. The origin of what happened that day was the common desire of two men for the power to be something they were never able to achieve. The outcome was political, social, historical. The suffering was all too human.

◆

From the moment he awoke in the Governor's Mansion in Montgomery, Alabama, on Monday, May 15, 1972, George Wallace was unusually nervous and irascible. He snapped at Cornelia and argued over the breakfast table with Peggy Sue, his second-oldest daughter, who was living with them while finishing her senior year at Troy State. The spat was over who got first dibs on the morning newspaper.[4]

There was no apparent reason for such edginess. The morning was soft and sunny. George Wallace had every right to fire up one of his omnipresent cigars, kick back, and contemplate his considerable achievements so far.

He had four hundred delegates in his pocket for the Democratic convention in Miami Beach in July. In addition, the polls now gave him a significant lead over his main rivals, Senators Hubert Humphrey and George McGovern, in the Maryland and Michigan primaries that would be held the following day.

True, this was not hard support. Most of his delegates were obligated to vote for Wallace on the first ballot only. They were free to negotiate a switch to one of the other candidates on the second ballot. That is, if there was a second ballot. Doubtful. That made his delegates restive and worried. There was no way Wallace could win the nomination, and they didn't want to be left out in the political cold when the winner's votes were counted. Most of them were McGovern or Humphrey people, anyway.

But Wallace's rivals were worried too. No one in those days ever expected a Southern politician to win as much support in the North as Wallace apparently had. His charisma and, worse, his ideas, were touching the blue-collar voters in the industrial north.

Wallace was telling them, I'm one of you, I know

what's on your minds and in your feelings, I'm your man and I'll fight for you. And they were listening to him. So a concerned Humphrey was taking this last day to campaign in Baltimore, while McGovern, wanting to make a good showing in his native Midwest, was on the hustings in Michigan.

But instead of feeling on top of the world, Wallace was uneasy and then some. He didn't really want to make the trip north today. By the eve of an election, a politician can do little more than show a confident, smiling face on television, predict victory not for himself but for the people, and fidget through the hours until the outcome is decided.

However, Wallace was prisoner of a last-day schedule that was already in motion. He and Cornelia were due to leave shortly for a full day of campaigning in Maryland, where he was set to appear at shopping center rallies in Wheaton and Laurel, followed in Glen Burry by a fund-raising dinner at twenty-five dollars a plate. The day would wind up with a boisterous rally at the National Guard Armory in Annapolis.

Still, he was tempted to make the Secret Service happy and cancel out. Why, when he had a commanding lead, risk a possible hostile confrontation with the press at the last minute or endure yet another face-off with demonstrators who had bedeviled all but two of his campaign stops in Maryland?

Agents assigned to protect the Alabama governor were touchy about shopping centers, always the most exposed and dangerous places for a candidate to show himself. On this trip, the Secret Service was especially concerned about Laurel, where their information indicated they could expect a belligerent crowd.

The assassinations of civil rights leader Medgar Evers, the enigmatic Malcolm X, American Nazi George Lincoln Rockwell, John and Robert Kennedy, and the Rev. Dr. Martin Luther King, Jr., were more than enough proof of the dangers that political figures risked by appearing in front of their publics. What's more, George Wallace seemed to attract louder and more violent troublemakers than any of his rivals.

At rallies throughout the Maryland campaign, most of the people who came out appeared to be on his side. But hecklers—the young, the bearded, and the angry—invariably seeped into the front rows at Wallace rallies, where they would try to outshout him and throw vegetables, rocks, and bottles to force him off the podium. They greeted him with bobbing middle fingers and chants of "Bullshit! Bullshit!" and "Hey, Gaaawdge! Fuck you, Gaaawdge!"

Wallace understood that the public had little tolerance for such modes of expression. The very excesses of his opposition made him look good by comparison. So he happily goaded them on. "Go ahead, throw something else," he taunted. "I can take anything you anarchists dish out."

Another favorite jibe: "Why don't y'all get a haircut?" This drove his long-haired antagonists to animal howls of frustration and at the same time played well to the larger audience, many of whom were fruitlessly trying to get their own children to do just that.[5]

Although Wallace, like most prominent politicians, was aware that of the thousands of eyes locked onto him wherever he appeared, some burned with hate and madness and others were icy with conspiratorial calculation, he remained fatalistic about the risks. This does not mean he was indifferent to them. The tomatoes and eggs thrown at him from close range were more of an annoyance than an outright danger. But rocks, pieces of metal, and even pennies, nasty little missiles, were another matter. The worst was called "soaping." This involved pushing nails through bars of soap and lobbing them, pointed ends out, at a speaker.

Wallace was a magnet for this type of artillery. His security men had to interpose their bodies between the candidate and the flying objects to deflect them as best they could. Since Wallace ignored the Secret Service's urging to stop campaigning at shopping centers, his protectors insisted that his staff cart around an eight-hundred-pound bulletproof lectern. At the Service's insistence, he also tried on a bulletproof vest. But the thing was so bulky that it hampered his movements in crowds and he quickly discarded it. [6]

Wallace's friends and family likewise worried about him. "George," said one crony, "you keep on and someone's going to shoot you." His young son, George Jr., once asked him about the dangers of running for the presidency. Wallace tried to minimize them. But little George remained unconvinced. Only days earlier, while accompanying Wallace on a campaign trip to Maryland, he dreamed that his father was shot in the throat and killed.[7]

Despite the dangers, an American politician cannot hope to win by revealing any fear of the public. He has to risk himself.

No one appreciated this fact better than Wallace. Besides, he was a people junkie. He loved to wade into crowds, shake hands, and ask for votes. As a passionate orator from the region where passionate oratory is an established art form, he had developed himself into a great stump speaker in the Huey Long mold. He argued, he thundered, he swaggered, he excoriated with rough humor, he cajoled, he pointed with alarm, and beckoned with hope. The podium was his true home. Accustomed as politicians are to public speaking, few of them could match George Wallace's ability to draw an audience to himself and play on its emotions like the pipes of Pan.

Most of us may inwardly quake at the thought of standing in front of thousands of screaming people and orating at them, telling them what they should believe, feel, and do, pumping them up until they are ready to burst.

But to Wallace, this was food. To hear an audience spontaneously cheer you, chant your name over and over like a mantra, *need* you, need you to think for them, feel for them, be for them, need you to verify them by putting their inchoate feelings into words, need you to be out there in front to lead them to the promised land of your personal vision, this is an experience of the viscera and it can be highly addictive. It makes you want to touch, embrace, connect through eyes, voice, and the pressure of hands. When you live life on this level, a simple handshake becomes a shared understanding, a bond, a reciprocal recognition, a promise to be honored.

To be a total politician, as Wallace was, is to know all this in your belly. And to know it is to need it.

So Wallace, despite his jittery state of mind and the feeling that he should stay home that day, instead allowed himself to be shoved onward by the unyielding schedule. He was annoyed at his press secretary, Billy Joe Camp, for setting up the Laurel appearance. But the thing was done and he did not want to disappoint the people who expected him.[8]

After his usual breakfast of orange juice, bacon, grits, and eggs buried under ketchup—but no biscuits this morning because "I'm getting fat,"—and a run through some newspapers, Wallace, still in his scarlet bathrobe, went upstairs. He found Cornelia under her hair dryer and grumped, "If you make me late, I'm going to leave without you." Then he disappeared into the bathroom to shave.[9]

From experience, Cornelia knew that politicians hate any surprises, such as a wife's unexpected washing of her hair, that could cause delays to the almighty schedule. She understood that everything is planned to the minute. Candidates running behind their schedules risk offending local dignitaries and supporters enslaved by their own schedules.

Neither are audiences pleased to be kept waiting. The curious might lose interest and even the convinced could wonder how you can run the country if you can't get to a simple shopping center on time.

Although she was inclined to stretch timetables to the snapping point, Cornelia was determined not to be left behind this day. She decided to skip breakfast, her favorite meal, and to leave for the airport with her hair unfinished.

The pace picked up. Wallace's shave was interrupted by a call from Camp. He wanted Cornelia to appear on a Washington television show while the governor went on to the Wheaton rally. Cornelia refused. She would stay with her husband. Camp also told Wallace that there were several requests for interviews between the rallies, but both men decided not to tempt fate with any more exposure to the press.

Wallace again expressed misgivings about the two outdoor rallies. "I've got a good mind to cancel," he said. But his press secretary insisted it would make Wallace look bad and again the governor reluctantly agreed to go ahead.

While Cornelia raced into a yellow dress and hastily made up, Wallace went to her downstairs office to make some last minute calls. Her secretary, Joanne Walker, offered to dial for him, but he grabbed for the phone and, in his nervousness, knocked it into a wastebasket. As he was finishing his last call, Cornelia appeared, ready to go. Wallace asked her if his tie matched his blue suit. She assured him it did.

At nine o'clock they left by the kitchen door. "We'll see y'all Wednesday," Wallace called out to the prison trustees who took care of the grounds. They waved back and wished him luck.

The Wallaces rode to the airport in silence. Their chartered Jet Commander was standing outside its hangar, but the two pilots were nowhere to be seen. While the party waited in the car, security men checked around and discovered that the pilots were still asleep in a nearby motel. The Wheaton and Laurel rallies had been added to Wallace's itinerary only a few days earlier and no one had remembered to tell them. This meant at least an hour's delay for the pilots to dress, get to the plane, check it out, and file a flight plan to Washington.

Wallace, who rarely lost his temper over mistakes made by others, decided to wait in a hangar office, where he calmly took a seat and lit a cigar. He withdrew into himself for a while and finally said to Cornelia, "I believe I won't go. If I haven't already won those two primaries, it's too late. I just believe I won't go." But the schedule was master of events and its momentum carried Wallace onto the plane and into the air.

Little was said during the flight to Washington's National Airport. Wallace didn't have to rehearse his remarks. Every politician has an all-purpose campaign pattern speech committed to memory. The speech is a compendium of his basic themes. Its language is refined over years in thousands of appearances at armories, Rotary and Kiwanis meetings, American Legion and VFW halls, picnics,

Fourth of July celebrations, county and state fairs, and anywhere else that large congregations wait to be sermonized. The lines have been tested and perfected: introductory lines; thank you lines; laugh lines; applause lines; lines to stir passion, patriotism, outrage, and faith; squelch lines for hecklers; and, lastly, get-off lines designed to leave them cheering.

What's more, the pattern speech is modular: a skilled practitioner can pull out different parts and retrofit them into short, extemporaneous talks or even a one-on-one, arm-around-the-shoulder conversation with a wealthy supporter or local party chieftain.

Wallace's pattern speech was sharpened to the point where it could draw blood, and frequently did. He used it to slash at the enemies of decent, respectable, working folk, citizens who obeyed the law, paid their taxes and labored for a better life, only to watch their own government erode everything they worked so hard for. And it was all the fault of those pointy-headed liberal intellectuals pulling the strings in Washington, telling people what they may and may not do. They were seizing control of American life, right down to the neighborhood schools.

Ah, schools! The key word. The Great American Threat of the sixties. Mention schools and everybody understood you were talking about busing between school districts to create a numerical racial balance intended to achieve court-ordered equality of education for Negro children.

But busing was an idea whose time would never really come. The issue touched too many raw nerves. People wanted their children to go to neighborhood schools and they wanted some say over what those schools taught and what they cost. They would fight any attempt to change that. Even those who wanted something done about the plight of Negroes, their decaying schools, their bleak past and unpromising future, drew the line at busing.

In the suburbs of cities like Detroit and Newark, the prospect that their children might be bused into inner-city schools to mix with black kids waiting with guns, knives, drugs, and hate, was enough to strike genuine terror into the hearts of both whites and upscale blacks who had worked to get out of the ghetto. And they were being told that anyone who opposed busing was at best a crypto-racist. The inner-city busing fear had its roots in an earlier court-ordered ruling in Michigan that was subsequently overturned. But the ruling did serve to induce tremors about just how far the courts were prepared to go and what the consequences could be.

Wallace was the first major politician to realize that the busing issue cut across class and economic lines in every region of the country and was creating a fear of the judiciary. He brought the issue north and flayed the "so-called intellectuals" and judges who made and supported this policy.

Wallace hammered at them in speech after speech.

They can afford to send their own children to pri-

vate schools while yours get bused to the inner city. They don't think you're smart enough or good enough or important enough to run your own schools. They think they know better than you do. They want to put your kids in buses and take them all over hell's half-acre just to meet some artificial enrollment numbers that they, not you, think is right.

They're not a bit better than you are, with all their phony college degrees and ten-syllable words. You're as good as anyone. You're the voters. You have the real power. You can call the shots by electing someone who'll stand up for you. Well, vote for Wallace and we'll show 'em who's in charge! Let's send 'em a message!

And, indeed, the shouting, whistling response by voters *was* a message. People cheered the aggressive little governor, with his dark eyebrows and flashing eyes, his angry Edward G. Robinson mouth pulled down at the corners, his chopping gestures and his apparent eagerness to carry the battle to anybody, in any position, at any time.

And many were voting to send his message. He might not get the nomination for president, but he would bring that message, endorsed by millions of voters, to the Democratic convention. George Wallace, who had been too poor to buy his own books in college, would be heard. With respect.

Wallace was still deep inside himself during the short drive out of Washington. His small entourage, consisting of Cornelia; Camp; Captain E.C. Dothard, his beefy personal bodyguard from the Alabama state police; and some aides and other state troopers, was now augmented by about twenty Secret

Service men as well as Maryland and Prince George's County uniformed and plainclothes police. Ahead raced a contingent of TV and print journalists.

Now that things were in motion, Wallace's pulse quickened and his mood grew lighter. The born campaigner with the inexhaustible memory was where he belonged, out carrying the fire. He looked across the seat at Cornelia and winked.[10]

At the Wheaton Shopping Center, the noontime air was hot and heavy under dark clouds. The delay in leaving Montgomery had left a large dent in the schedule. Some three thousand people were gathered and many were in a sour mood.

Wallace's bulletproof lectern was on the speaker's platform, a flatbed truck trailer decorated with red, white, and blue bunting. Flatbeds are an ideal temporary platform for such rallies. They can be rented from a local contractor, set up quickly, and camouflaged with patriotic decorations. They are able to hold upwards of fifty politicos and guests in easy view of a large audience. When the rally is over, the trailers are towed away and commercial life returns to normal.

Shortly before the motorcade pulled up next to the trailer, reporters and photographers arrived to set up their cameras and survey the crowd. One of the cameramen was Laurens W. Pierce, a longtime CBS photographer who had flown up from his home near Atlanta that morning to cover Wallace's last day of campaigning in Maryland.

Pierce was panning his 16-mm Auricon sound

camera over the crowd when he saw a familiar figure standing close to the platform. He had noticed the young man at previous rallies. He was about five feet six inches tall, not quite Wallace's height, with close-cropped white-reddish hair.

Typically, the man was wearing a red and white striped shirt, a dark tie, charcoal jacket with large Wallace buttons above the lapels, dark pants, and clip-on sunglasses. A chilling smile was the most arresting thing about him. It was a strange, inward kind of knowing smile, almost a smirk. Pierce also had been intrigued by the man's bizarre behavior. He had cheered and applauded everything Wallace said with such outlandish zeal that it attracted attention. On a previous occasion, Pierce had swung his 95-mm zoom lens around and filmed him.[11]

On impulse, Pierce left his camera on its tripod and strolled over to the man. "I've photographed you at other rallies," he said. The smile vanished. The blond man shook his head and edged quickly away. Nonplused, Pierce returned to his camera, wondering if in some way he had offended this strange character.

The young man moved on and later asked a policemen to get Wallace to come over and shake his hand. The cop didn't bother to answer. He asked the same favor of a Secret Service agent but was likewise ignored.[12]

Wallace pulled up minutes later and quickly got out of the car, Cornelia at his heels. Ordinarily, Cornelia was introduced first so that Wallace wouldn't have to break his speaking stride to do it later. Few people knew that she had phlebitis and the inflamed veins in her legs made prolonged sitting with bent knees an agony. She frequently had to leave before Wallace finished speaking.

As she moved toward the platform, a local politician stopped her. "That crowd looks pretty rough," he told her. "We'd prefer that you didn't go out on the stage." Since she had been unable to get her hair arranged properly, Cornelia felt it was just as well to be out of the limelight.[13]

The politician's instincts proved to be accurate. The rally was a disaster. Hardly had Wallace stepped in front of the microphones when curses filled the air, along with rocks, tomatoes, and bars of soap bristling with nails. Wallace's security men grabbed posters to ward off the barrage while he peered over the lectern and heckled the demonstrators. "Your vocabulary is mighty limited if all you can say are nasty words like that," he told them.[14]

The situation went quickly out of control. There was no use prolonging it. Wallace cut his speech short and ducked into his car. The convoy re-formed and pulled out of the shopping center for Laurel. The young man with the Wallace buttons walked back to his car, a weary blue Rambler Rebel with Wisconsin plates, and drove out of the shopping center.

At Laurel, Wallace's motorcade went to the Howard Johnson motel, where layover rooms had been taken. Everyone planned to freshen up and have lunch before leaving for the three o'clock rally at the Laurel Oak Shopping Center. Cornelia made arrangements to have her hair combed out by a local beautician at two o'clock.

At about one-thirty, the Wallaces, accompanied by Camp, Dothard, another Alabama security man, two Maryland troopers, and the full complement of Secret Service agents, went to a large meeting room in the motel for lunch.

Wallace had his preferred meal: chopped steak awash in ketchup and large glasses of milk and iced tea. Cornelia left early for her hairdresser appointment, accompanied by one of the Maryland troopers. By the time her hair was set, teased, and combed out, it was past time for the rally to begin.

Swinging back by the motel, she saw that the motorcade had left without her. This was not a surprise. Cornelia understood that Wallace would never be late for a rally if he could help it, so she and the trooper continued on to the nearby mall. They arrived after Wallace was well into his speech.

The Laurel Oak Shopping Center was the only major one in the area at that time. Separate stores with a long common roof were squared off around three sides of a large parking lot. Facing them from the open side was a small, one-story branch office of the Equitable Trust Bank. Wallace's bulletproof podium had been eased down from a truck in front of the bank and placed under a large canvas canopy that had been erected to shield the speaker from rain. The weather was still muggy and cloudy, but brightening.

The Wheaton fiasco, added to memories of snarling demonstrators at other shopping centers, made the security people even more tense and alert. Policemen with shotguns paced on the roofs over the stores. State, county, and Laurel plainclothesmen mingled with a crowd that had been gathering since noon around another flatbed trailer, also festooned with patriotic bunting. Billy Grammar and his country-and-western Gotta Travel On Boys band twanged out their theme song, "I've Gotta Travel On." By three o'clock, a thousand people were gathered behind the ropes that marked off the VIP and press areas.[15]

Gilbert Roland Saunders, his wife, Madeline, and their three young children had a splendid viewing position at the rope to the speaker's left. The Saunders had been Wallace supporters for years, and this time they were both working for the candidate's organization in town. They wanted to meet the man, shake his hand, and personally wish him well.

Close by were fellow campaign workers Ross and Mabel Speigel and Mrs. Speigel's mother, all sporting Wallace buttons and plastic boaters. Speigel, a crane operator, also wanted to look into Wallace's eye, shake his hand, and promise the governor his family's support.[16]

The onlookers stirred with excitement as press vehicles arrived and reporters set themselves up. This is always a glamorous moment for the spectators, but for the average newsman it is just another dull routine. Reporters who follow candidates get to learn every line of the pattern speech and eventually just close their ears in boredom. For the most part, they attend such functions to assess crowd reactions and to cover anything out of the ordinary that might happen.

Radio reporter Val Hymes, who also wrote a column for several weekly newspapers in the area, stood by as some of her colleagues decided to leave early. She elected to stay, telling the others that she was not so much interested in the speech as in what was happening to Wallace as a candidate. "What could happen that's new?" another reporter asked. "Well," she answered, "he might get shot."[17]

The three small Saunders children became restless. Mrs. Saunders took them to a drugstore for a Coke and a visit to the restrooms. When she returned to her place at the rope, the young blond man with the constant, secret smile was there. He looked at the children. "Do you like Wallace?" he asked. One of the boys said he guessed he did. "Why?" persisted the man. "What do you like about him?"[18]

Just then, the Wallace caravan pulled into the parking lot and came along the right side of the bank by the entrance. Applause broke out. The young man cheered and clapped louder than anyone.

After greeting the local party leaders, Wallace was led to the flag-draped podium to address the crowd. This audience was nothing like the one at Wheaton. A few hecklers jeered "Geeoorge!" but they were in the minority. This crowd was friendly and receptive. Like the Saunders and Speigels, they were blue-collar people who liked Wallace.

With his head, shoulders, and jabbing fingers visible above the podium, Wallace launched into the fifteen-minute version of his set piece about the "pluperfect hypocrisy" of establishment politicians who so badly misperceived true American values. He railed at the influence of "intellectual morons" at universities who couldn't even "park their bicycles straight." He spoke about law and order and muggers in Washington who get out of jail before their victims get out of the hospital. "Why, somebody could be knocked in the head as they walk away from this shopping center today!" he cried.

Shortly after Cornelia arrived, Wallace's voice developed a harshness and he began to cough. Cornelia knew the signs of strained vocal cords and she knew a good cure, too. She sent an aide running to a nearby grocery store for a jar of honey. When he returned, she tore off the top of a Styrofoam coffee cup and filled the remaining part with honey.

"Take this to the governor and tell him to drink it," she ordered. The aide passed it up to Wallace with a whispered "Your wife said to drink it." Apparently unwilling to break his rhythm, Wallace put the cup aside untouched but did manage to get more power into his voice.

Some honey stuck to Cornelia's fingers. The bank would have a washroom. She rapped on the glass entrance until a woman employee opened it. Cornelia asked for a place to wash her hands and was taken to the ladies' room. As she cleaned up, the woman mentioned that she wanted to meet

Wallace but had been told to stay inside the building. "Come to the door when he stops speaking," Cornelia urged. "I'll come over and get you so you can meet him."[19]

By the time she returned, Wallace was booming the applause lines. "Vote tomorrow and shake the eye-teeth of the Democratic party," he shouted. "Tell 'em a vote for George Wallace is a vote for the average citizen! Let's give 'em a case of St. Vitus Dance! Let's send 'em a message!"

The crowd loved it all and responded with cheers. As the governor waved and grinned, the sun broke through the clouds. Then he walked down several steps in the middle of the platform, where two women from his Laurel campaign headquarters were waiting to embrace him and give him a peck on the cheek. One of them was Dora Thompson, who was to run as a Wallace delegate four years later.

Wallace autographed a couple of pictures and exchanged some remarks with the officials. Then he turned quickly toward the waiting cars at his right. But the onlookers wouldn't release him. They applauded and called him back to shake hands. "Over here!" the smiling man kept shouting from his place by the Speigels. "George, over here!"

Wallace's political instincts took over. He shucked off his suit jacket, gave it to an aide and headed back to the crowd with three security men at his side. These were E.C. Dothard and Secret Service agents Nicholas Zarvos and Jimmy Taylor. More comfortable now in his light blue, short-sleeved shirt, the candidate approached his fans.

Politicians usually work a crowd from left to right so that they can easily shake hands. Wallace followed the same route, smiling, acknowledging each individual and pumping every outstretched hand.

After filming the speech, Pierce stepped out of the security area and followed along, filming over Wallace's shoulder. He saw someone tap Wallace to get his attention. The tap was repeated a moment later and Wallace turned back to his left.[20]

When Pierce moved in front of her, Cornelia lost sight of her husband, even though he was only about a yard away. Dora Thompson walked up and introduced herself. Cornelia smiled and immediately remembered the woman in the bank. Turning her back to the crowd, Cornelia saw her among the people waiting by the door.

At that moment, an arm flashed between the Speigels, pointing a small, snub-nosed revolver. It went right past Madeline Saunders' face as she was being jostled by the excited crowd. Wallace was saying, "Thank you and tell—" [21]

Pop-pop-pop-pop-pop! The sound was like small balloons bursting. Madeline Saunders and Ross Speigel grabbed the arm holding the gun. Speigel tried to push it up while she pulled it down.

From his vantage point behind Wallace, Pierce thought at first that someone had set off a string of firecrackers. Then he saw the gun being fired at Wallace, who was almost in front of him. Pierce kept filming as Wallace was knocked to the asphalt at his feet, in shock but conscious. Seeing a flurry of activity in his viewfinder, Pierce focused on that, filmed Nick Zarvos clutching his throat, then pulled back and aimed his camera down at Wallace, who lay with blood coming out the right side of his chest.[22]

Nearby, Dothard held his stomach. Dora Thompson did not at first feel the shattered bone in her right calf. She staggered for a few steps and abruptly sat down.

Agent Zarvos bent over and vomited blood. A bullet had hit the right side of his jaw, zipped around through his throat to sever some of his vocal cords and lodged in his left jaw, fracturing it and knocking out several teeth.[23]

For Cornelia, all motion stopped. Her thoughts were clear and oddly analytical. The first three shots seemed to come from her right and the last two from the left. She concluded that two people were firing. She turned and saw Wallace flat on his back, his left arm flung out and his knees bent to the left, a spreading red stain above his waist on the right side. No one was near him. No one was moving. Her mind continued to work smoothly. He wasn't dead. She had a chance to save him before another gunman finished him off on the ground. To do that, she decided to die.

As slowly as everything was moving for her, it took only six seconds after the shooting for Cornelia to reach Wallace. She flung herself on him, trying to cover his body with hers. Archie Cook, a young plainclothesman with the Laurel Police and later its chief, moved to knock her out of the way. Almost instinctively, he too was expecting a second gunman, which could just as well be a woman. "It's his wife," another cop yelled at Cook. "You stay with her and I'll stay with him."[24]

Enraged, people jumped on the assailant. "Kill the son of a bitch!" someone shouted. As the blond young man went down under the combined weight of Speigel, Saunders, other bystanders, and police, his smile was finally gone.

Eyes in the Body

ARTHUR HERMAN BREMER, AN INTROSPEC-
tive, hypersensitive, 21-year-old psychopath from
Milwaukee, shopped carefully before selecting the
revolver with which he initially intended to kill
President Richard M. Nixon, before changing his
target to George Wallace.

He rejected buying one of the cheap handguns
popularly known as Saturday Night Specials. Their
availability was an unintended result of the Omni-
bus Crime Bill of 1968. Enacted after Robert F.
Kennedy's assassination, this bill prohibited the im-
portation of foreign handguns. The law was legally
circumvented by importers who simply brought in
stamped components made of low-cost metal alloys
and assembled them in major cities, principally
Miami, Florida. Saturday Night Specials are neither
reliable nor accurate, although accuracy is not a
prime requisite for close-in use. The parts fit so
poorly that malfunctions are fairly routine. Bullets
have been known to shatter between a misaligned
cylinder and barrel, spewing out hot slivers of steel,
or even at times to explode.[25]

That would not do for Bremer. He appreciated

the difficulties of getting past the walls of Secret Service agents that surround a candidate. If he could do it, he wanted no malfunctions. His life was one big malfunction as it was, but when it came to assassination, he needed quality weapons to be successful. Above all, he burned to be successful.

So he purchased two high-quality handguns: a 9 mm Browning automatic with a fourteen-shot clip and a revolver of comparable power, a blunt, ugly little stopper named Undercover II, manufactured by the Charter Arms Company of Stratford, Connecticut.

Undercover II holds five .38-caliber cartridges, the same size used by most police departments. It is extremely accurate and can be fired as fast as the trigger is pulled. Most importantly, it is so small that with its one and seven-eighths inch barrel, the length Bremer chose, it can easily be concealed in a man's hand. It is, as the name implies, designed for undercover police work. Bremer carried it in his right jacket pocket.[26]

It takes less than a thousandth of a second for a bullet to be fired. The hammer strikes a soft metal cap containing primer, a pinhead of shock-sensitive explosive material. The explosion of the primer sets the nitrocellulose in the gunpowder on fire. The burning powder releases water and an immense volume of carbon dioxide that builds up pressure and pops the bullet out of its casing like a cork from a champagne bottle. Rifling, spiral grooves inside the barrel, sets the bullet spinning, usually one revolution every sixteen inches. This gives it directional stability and prevents it from tumbling through the air. It also makes the bullet burrow into its target like an electric drill. In the approximately three feet between Bremer and Wallace, each bullet spun about two and one-quarter times before screwing itself, at the speed of 750 feet per second, into Wallace's body.[27]

The governor was shot at least four times and possibly five. Since he was facing slightly to the left, in relation to Bremer, one bullet passed through his upper right arm and another through the right forearm. One or both of these bullets may have continued into the body. Wallace's right shoulder blade was deeply grazed and there was another flesh wound on the front of the right shoulder.[28]

These shots did no serious permanent damage. But two others did. The first was more immediately life-threatening. The second did the worst long-term harm. The first of these bullets, which perhaps was one of the two that passed through his right arm, corkscrewed into Wallace's stomach, splattering half-digested bits of chopped steak throughout the abdominal cavity. Wallace's colon also was nicked. If it had been penetrated, the bowel contents would likewise have poured into the abdomen and caused much more critical infections than the food particles were to do. Wallace escaped this fate by a fraction of an inch.

The second bullet entered his body in the flank area under the right rib. It twisted through the erector spinae muscle group and lodged in the foramen, an opening in the side of the spine, between the thoracic twelve and lumbar one vertebra, five vertebrae up from the base of the spine.

There it stopped, pressed nose down against the bottom of the spinal cord which ends one vertebra lower. Below that is the cauda equina, the "horse's tail" of nerves at the base of the spine, which was untouched. If the bullet had gone about one inch lower, it would have hit these nerves instead of the spinal cord. In such a case, Wallace might eventually have recovered, because severed nerve ends can regenerate. A damaged spinal cord never does. If the bullet had been about one-half inch higher, it would likely have struck a pedicle, the bony knob that can be felt through the skin over the spine. Assuming that it did not penetrate this bone—there was no bone damage where it did hit—Wallace could also have avoided paralysis.

As for the spinal cord itself, the bullet did not hit with enough force to sever it. But the spinal cord was so badly bruised that it would never recover. Wallace became an instant paraplegic.[29]

The governor was alive, but assassinated. His career as a national political leader, the career that was the breath of life to him, his very essence, was murdered on the Laurel Oaks blacktop. This was Wallace's first, and in some ways hardest, death. He would live on more than twenty years and never again spend a day without pain. He was fifty-two years old.

In the end, it was Bremer's message, hidden all his life behind a knowing smirk, that was delivered.

II

The 'Whild Thing'

LEE HARVEY OSWALD AND JOHN F. KENNEDY. Sirhan B. Sirhan and Robert F. Kennedy. James Earl Ray and Martin Luther King, Jr., Sara Jane Moore and Gerald Ford. John Hinckley, Jr., and Ronald Reagan. Arthur Herman Bremer and George Corley Wallace.

The list of modern American political assassins and their quarries is short. Not all were successful in terms of killing their intended victim. Moore's bullet missed Ford. Hinckley shot Reagan and his press secretary, James Brady, with a small-bore pistol. Had Hinckley used a weapon with the throw weight of Bremer's, Reagan likely would have become the third president to be assassinated in this century, after William McKinley in 1901 and John F. Kennedy in 1963. Brady, permanently disabled with a head wound, would not have survived either. Bremer put Wallace in a wheelchair for life and wounded three other people in the process.

But all of these assassins were highly successful in other terms. They altered the country's contemporary history and made people wonder if the political process was becoming untracked. They caused America and its friends and enemies alike to question the nation's character, stability, and direction. They generated frustration and fear and convinced some politicians to at least rethink the perils of running for national office. They caused pain and tragedy. And the attempt made by each one was inspiration for others.

Information and insights about these shadowy figures are sketchy. Psychologists have amassed enough information to draw mental profiles and find correlations between the personalities of modern assassins. Oswald and Bremer, for example, were raised by stifling mothers in cramped quarters, in intellectually, psychologically, and culturally impoverished environments. Both had grandiose ideas about themselves to match their self-loathing.

But profiles and correlations appear somewhat superficial in light of the ultimate question: Why? Why did they actually *do* it, instead of dreaming about it or making a fatal but avoidable mistake that gave their plans away, or calling the whole scheme off for one reason or another? Why were these few particular people the ones to persevere in the face of all kinds of barriers, blunders, and discouragements until they finally had their opportunity to pull the trigger, and did?

In all likelihood, this ultimate question will never be fully answered, psychological insights notwithstanding. The inner landscape of each person's soul and being, his contact with humanity, his imaginings, delusions, illusions, and ability to feel for something other than himself, are too hazy and remote to be seen clearly through today's psychological lenses. We simply do not understand ourselves all that well. Especially, we do not understand those among us whose minds have been taken over by the basest of all obsessions, the need to destroy another human being, and who have the will to actually make the attempt.

All the same, because assassins have figured so prominently in twentieth-century American political life, it is worth asking this most fundamental question and examining such evidence as exists, with Bremer as our example, if only to get some sense of what it might mean to be an assassin. What does the assassin think? What does he feel? What animates him? In Bremer's case, we have his diaries and the records of psychologists. But the ultimate question will still stand, enticing, beckoning from a great distance behind Arthur Bremer's dreadful smile. Why? In fact—not in theory—why?

◆

Bremer was pulled from the crowd's grasp by Corporal Michael M. Landrum of the Prince George's County Police Department. A half-dozen other Prince George's policemen surrounded them.

Dragging Bremer in armlocks and headlocks, they fought their way clear of hysterical people who were punching them as well as Bremer and grabbing for their service revolvers in order to kill him.

The county police cars were locked, so they

pushed Bremer into a state police cruiser and drove quickly out of the parking lot.

They made sure that his cuts and bruises were treated quickly. A local doctor sutured a gash in his head, which was bloodied by Wallace supporters trying to pound it into the pavement. Special Agent Thomas H. Farrow of the FBI placed him under arrest at 8:30 that night and charged him with attempted murder, assault with intent to murder, assault with intent to maim, assault and battery, and carrying and using a handgun.

Benjamin Lipsitz, an attorney from Baltimore, arrived with an appointment from U.S. Magistrate Clarence E. Goetz to represent Bremer, who had only $1.55 to his name.

Lipsitz already knew that Bremer's defense would have to be based on temporary insanity. Before Bremer was taken to the Baltimore County Jail at Towson to be lodged for the night, Lipsitz gave him a password, "Socrates," the name of Lipsitz's dog. The lawyer told Bremer he could safely talk to anyone who gave that password, such as a defense investigator or psychiatrist. Otherwise, Bremer was to say nothing to anybody. Lipsitz needed time to organize his case, line up expert witnesses to reinforce the insanity defense and prepare Bremer for the psychological examinations that would start soon.

Psychology recognizes mental disorders but not insanity as such. Insanity is a legal concept, not a medical term. The purpose of insanity in law is to establish culpability, to determine, in the words of

Maryland law, whether the accused "lacks substantial capacity either to appreciate the criminality of his conduct or to conform his conduct to the requirements of the law."

The issue is decided by a jury of men and women presumed to possess enough common sense and objectivity to find their way through a welter of conflicting testimony by prosecution and defense psychiatrists. These specialists work with essentially the same data developed through tests and interviews. It is their opinions that vary, in accordance with their experience, their judgment, and the requirements of the side that hires them. Their gut feelings about the accused are just as meaningful to them, perhaps even more so, as their interpretations of the standard psychiatric test data.

Jurors themselves need accurate gut feelings to decide which psychiatrists to believe. The whole idea of innocence by reason of insanity may be as suspect to them as to any skeptic. After all, who—mental health professionals or average citizens—can judge the matter with any degree of assurance that they are serving justice? But the law charges them with this responsibility and they must carry it out.

If the jury agrees with defense psychiatric witnesses, then the accused cannot be held responsible for the crime. In theory, he could be quickly released, but in practice this happens very rarely. He may be kept in preventive detention while undergoing treatment—and later freed—if psychiatrists agree he is rehabilitated and unlikely to commit another crime, and if the courts accept this finding. If psychiatrists determine that therapy is not effective, he may never be released.

If, on the other hand, the jury agrees with the prosecution's psychiatrists that the defendant did not lack the capacity, then he must, like any other sane convicted criminal, pay for his crime by spending a specified portion of his remaining years locked in a cage—assuming, in capital cases, that the court allows him any remaining years at all.

This dichotomy, a sure sentence for the sane but an indeterminate sentence for the insane, with no guarantee that someone who has been found insane could not be released at almost any time, troubles judges, attorneys, criminologists, the psychiatric profession, and an increasingly nervous public, no less than juries caught in the middle.

Not at all surprisingly, temporary insanity is the plea of choice for any killer who lacks an alibi or any hint of a mitigating circumstance. Convince a sympathetic judge or jury that you were mentally deranged during the slaughter in question but are feeling much more sociable now, even contrite, and you stand an excellent chance of avoiding dire punishment and perhaps eventually walking away free. It is not the most daunting challenge to find judges and jurors who are predisposed to accept that society, not the actual killer, is ultimately at fault for the crime.

But imperfect as it is, the insanity concept is one of the law's well-intentioned attempts to meld justice with mercy. It admits the possibility that some people are so far gone that they simply do not know what they are doing and cannot control themselves. A person firing at a president may think he is shooting Hitler or Stalin or the Devil incarnate.

Is it demonstrably impossible for any such person to respond to treatment, to disabuse himself of his delusions, or simply to outgrow them in time and try to make amends? The law cannot with absolute certainty prejudge this question. Without the insanity plea there would be no hope for those who have some chance to recover, few as they may be.

As Lipsitz began to construct his case, the press and law enforcement agencies, clinical psychologists and psychiatric social workers were uncovering the details of Bremer's sunless life. Their investigations rounded out a case study in genetic and environmental chaos.[30]

◆

Arthur Herman Bremer was born August 21, 1950, in the run-down South Side of Milwaukee, Wisconsin. The family was on the lower economic fringe and moved from one low-rent apartment to another.

Bremer's mother, Sylvia Imse Bremer, was born of a German immigrant family that was uneducated, violent, alcoholic, and, according to some psychiatric indications, possibly incestuous.[31]

She started her working life as a housecleaner at the age of eight. Sylvia had two illegitimate children, Gail, born in 1936, and Theodore, born the following year. She married William Bremer in

1939 while pregnant with his first son, William Jr. The couple waited eleven years before having Arthur. Their last child, Roger Dean, was born in 1954.

William Bremer was one of six children of a barber whose proudest boast was that he had fought in the Spanish-American War. At the age of nine, William was following a playmate through a wooded area when the boy let a thornapple branch snap back, hitting William in the face. He lost the sight of his right eye. Two years later, his mother suddenly became ill and died within forty-eight hours. William never recovered from this second blow. His schoolwork disintegrated to such an extent that he had to repeat several grades. He quit school as soon as he could and became a local truck driver.

William Bremer was a mild, well-meaning man who tried to provide some stability for the family. But he could not cope with his emotionally uncontrollable wife. Sylvia had a hair-trigger temper. She was given to throwing anything at hand, including knives, at the children when they bothered her. She periodically refused to prepare meals and, while obsessive about her children's personal hygiene, was a slovenly housekeeper. Her husband found solace in the neighborhood taverns.

Despite the riotous atmosphere, marked by parental tantrums, drinking bouts, harsh and inconsistent discipline, and their utter inability to understand their own or their children's needs, Sylvia and William Bremer remained steadfastly together.

There was nowhere else for either of them to go.

Arthur was the "good" boy, his mother's favorite. He was the only child who never got into trouble with the juvenile authorities. He was quiet—in fact, he didn't speak until he was four—docile and unthreatening.

He was also unresponsive. Young Arthur developed what the psychologists term a "shut-in personality." Teachers noted that he made no friends and did not join in the usual school activities. He smiled constantly under his growing internal pressures. It was the type of smile that psychiatrists often call "schizzy." One psychiatrist at Bremer's trial had a simpler term: a "shit-eatin' grin."

The jobs Arthur Bremer was to hold later, janitor, waiter and busboy, were similar to his mother's early ones in that they involved serving strangers and cleaning up after them.[32]

When he was ten years old, the family made another move. This one was sudden. It tore him sharply from a school environment in which he was beginning to feel secure. After that, his previous religious fervor abruptly dissolved. He left the Lutheran church, to which he had been strongly attached, and became obsessive about suicide. For months on end, he would plan his death in detail. On several occasions, to "gain relief," as he later expressed it to a psychiatrist, he went to nearby railroad tracks to lie down and let a train run over him. But he would change his mind or be dissuaded by the presence of nearby workmen.

Bremer regarded death as running away,

oblivion, with no rebirth in heaven. Ev
retained a feeling that there was some ki
nection between the living and the de_
pressed these contradictory viewpoints in one of
his later rambling poems about the joys, tortures
and boredoms of life. They are, he wrote, beyond
the wildest dreams of everyone living and yet to
live, while the joys, tortures, and boredoms of death
are equally beyond the wildest dreams of the dead.

In its own confused mode of expression, this is
life and death without meaning and, consequently,
without hope. Meaninglessness seems to have been
a real torment to him, and small wonder. A life without meaning is a life not worth living. The search
for meaning has animated poets, philosophers, and
theologians since the earliest ages, for they recognized that meaninglessness is a grave psychological affliction. Meaninglessness makes murder and
suicide plausible. Both were attractive to Bremer—
especially, at the beginning, suicide. After all, if life
has no meaning, then neither has death.

If not an early suicide, Bremer felt he would die
young of a brain tumor. He had several headaches
a week for more than ten years.[33]

At the age of eleven, he handed in a class assign-
ment so suspiciously off the mark that the teacher
ordered an IQ test and psychological evaluation.
Bremer was infuriated. He thought he had done a
good job. His IQ graded out at a subpar 92. His in-
appropriate smile was determined to be part of an
effort to keep disturbing feelings out of his mind
and a reflection of his intense daydreaming.

Bremer was unusually sensitive to any sign of rejection by other people. His school years were a special torture. The other children teased him unmercifully about his habit of mumbling to himself and that perpetual weird smile. They bestowed on him the hated nickname, "Clown."

Bremer knew he was different, but he tried as best he could to fight his growing sense of isolation. At South Division High School, he went out for football. He made the third-string team, but his mother, afraid he'd be hurt, forced him to quit.

So Arthur Bremer grew up to become a loner, a sullen masturbator who never dated girls, an eccentric with a shit-eatin' grin who buried himself in the apartment in front of the television set, dreaming of being a big shot in spite of his small physical stature.

After he graduated from high school, Bremer suddenly changed. The meek, neat, submissive boy turned into an irritable, sloppy, aggressive complainer. He hated the monotony and poor quality of the food at home and often refused to eat meals. He was constantly angry at Sylvia, dubbed her "the bitch" and accused her of being a bad mother. He demanded clean towels and washcloths several times a day and sheets and pillow cases two or three times a week. He was so insistent that Sylvia ended up buying new ones for him. Considering the family's lack of money, he became downright extravagant about clothes, complaining bitterly that his allowance was not enough to let him dress properly.[34]

About this time, he decided to become a writer. He enrolled as a full-time English major at Milwaukee Technical College. But Bremer never understood that college work requires students to be organized, take initiative, and stay up to speed on assignments. So at first, college seemed easy. Other than some reading, there appeared to be little to bother about. Then, seemingly all at once, he was inundated by examinations and immediate deadlines for papers and reports. Bremer found himself living the nightmare, often dreamed by college graduates, of walking into class and suddenly finding that a major examination was about to be given and not one book had been cracked. In a panic, he dropped out after only six weeks.

A year later, he went back to the same college to study photography. This too did not last long. He bought expensive equipment for the course and spent more than five hundred dollars for two cameras. He shot a great many pictures but they showed no artistic ability and he showed no enthusiasm. At the end of each class, he was the first one out the door.

Bremer held a series of low-level jobs. While still in high school he worked as a busboy at the Milwaukee Athletic Club. He also bused briefly at a restaurant called the Pieces of Eight and was a part-time janitor at the Story Elementary School.

At the athletic club, he was regarded as a good worker, although strange. He whistled, talked to himself, laughed at nothing discernible, and held pitchers of water high over the glasses while pouring. Because of this type of behavior, his supervisor moved him to a secondary dining room. The demotion enraged Bremer. He lodged an unfair labor practice complaint against his employer and sat grinning eerily throughout the hearing. He lost.

Life at home wasn't getting any easier. Arthur often argued violently with his father about the selection of television programs. During one dispute in October 1971, he hit his father in the face. The blow was not hard and the elder Bremer didn't retaliate. A few days later, Arthur rented a one-bedroom apartment about a mile away and left home permanently, just as all his older siblings had.

Sylvia Bremer was terribly upset. She tried repeatedly to contact him. She trudged to his apartment and left messages and food outside his door. But he never responded. On one occasion, she heard a radio inside but when she knocked it suddenly stopped. There was no answer.

During this period, Bremer met a high-school girl named Joan Pemrich, who worked part-time as a hall monitor at a recreation center in the Story Elementary School while Bremer was a janitor there.

Joan was fifteen years old, tall, slender and plain, a long-haired blonde who wore glasses. She was attracted to Bremer because he was older and, she assumed, more worldly than her contemporaries. As for Bremer, he was so entranced by her interest that he managed to reach out beyond his own walls to ask for a date. It was the first for both. He took her to a photography exhibit.

They had about five dates from Thanksgiving through mid-December of 1971. Those three weeks were the happiest of Bremer's life. He had a whole new sense of what a relationship with someone else could be. At work, he became more pleasant and cooperative. Things seemed finally to be turning for him.

But not for Joan. The relationship quickly became frightening. "He seemed to be getting awfully weird," she recalled. "He would just do goofy things, walk around goofy and say goofy things. People laughed at him all the time."

Once, when they were waiting in line to go to a rock concert, Bremer grabbed a passing teenage girl and kissed her hand. The girl screamed and called a policeman, who warned Bremer not to do it again. At the concert, Bremer became hyper. He bounced up and down and applauded wildly when no one else did. The people around him snickered. Goofy.[35]

Bremer was jealous of Joan's other friendships. He refused to speak to her girlfriends and had little if anything to say to her family. Claiming to be knowledgeable about psychology, he kept after Joan to open up and tell him her real feelings. He analyzed everything she said, finding meanings she never intended. He pressured her to study world history so she could understand global problems and thereby understand herself. He insisted that he wanted to help her overcome her personal hang-ups. Joan did not buy all this. It didn't take her long to realize who had the hang-ups.

Finally, his overanxious questioning about her

problems, his frightening stares, smoldering temper, and obscene talk became too much and she broke up with him.

Unbelieving, he kept after her at school, but she refused to speak to him. In an attempt to gain her sympathy, he shaved his head bald, leaving only his long sideburns. He wanted her to see that without her he was as empty inside as outside. Finding her in a school hall, he dramatically pulled his hat off. She just walked away.

Bremer was shattered. The door to the storybook land had been slammed and bolted in his face.

On January 13, he made one last attempt to call Joan, but her mother answered and told him to leave the girl alone.

On that same day, Bremer went to the Casanova gun store in Milwaukee. He bought the 9 mm Browning automatic and the .38-caliber Undercover II revolver, along with a supply of blunt-nosed semi-wadcutter bullets, so called because they cut a clean hole in paper targets to make scoring accurate.[36]

Around this time, Aziz Shihab, a reporter for the *San Antonio Express and News* received a call from someone who called himself "Art." Noting that Shihab had written a book about Sirhan Sirhan, the caller asked if Shihab felt a person was justified to kill if "his love fails or his girlfriend jilts him." Shihab acknowledged that such motives exist in the Middle East but added that he did not believe they were justified. He said he had made this attitude clear in his book. "Art" argued with him for a few minutes and then hung up.[37]

Bremer was fast slipping into the grip of a virtually irresistible urge to kill someone and be killed in return.

He concocted a plan to go to a downtown bridge during the evening rush hour with a noose around his neck. He would tie the free end of the rope to a railing, climb over and perch above the river. From this vantage point, clinging to the railing, he would take out his guns and shoot people indiscriminately. The last bullet would be fired into his own head. Even if he somehow survived this shot, he would still fall off the bridge and hang himself. If the rope happened to break, he would plunge into the freezing water and drown. And as an extra precaution to ensure his own death, he would first overdose on some kind of sleeping pills.

Bremer wrote the word "Killer" on his forehead with a blue felt tip pen, pulled a knit cap over his head, draped the noose around his neck, wound the rope around his waist, and headed downtown. He had the revolver in one pocket and the automatic in another and carried a bag of bullets.

Before going to the bridge, he stopped at a fast food restaurant for a last meal. The place was hot but Bremer could not take off his hat or coat for fear of revealing the message on his forehead or the noose coiled around his neck and body. So he remained tightly under wraps, the sack of bullets at his feet, eating his final dinner in a clinging steambath of sweat. He swallowed twelve Sominex tablets during the dinner.

Then something unexpected happened. A waitress smiled and spoke pleasantly to him. Caught off guard, Bremer left her a tip larger than the cost of the meal. He then walked to the edge of the bridge. While he waited for the homeward rush hour to build up, the waitress finished her shift and walked past. Still glowing from the large tip, she again smiled at him. Bremer's plan collapsed on the spot. He could not kill anyone at that place after she had been so nice to him. He trudged home. The Sominex did not even make him sleepy.

After that, he began to disappear. He disappeared from his last job, at the Story school, in February 1972. He disappeared from any family contacts and familiar haunts. He disappeared into his new persona, which he was to title "Assassinator."

◆

In August 1980, Sherman Griffin, a construction worker, was running his grader through a landfill, digging footings as part of a repair project on Milwaukee's 27th Street viaduct that crosses the Menomonee Valley. In the process, he unearthed a cheap briefcase. He didn't think too much about it at first. Lost or discarded objects, the detritus of people's lives, were frequently uncovered during excavations.[38]

But something about the briefcase held his attention. Throughout the day, he kept looking back at it. Finally, he got off the grader and opened it. Inside was a package tightly wrapped with protective aluminum foil and bound with masking tape.

Griffin stripped off this covering and found an ordinary school composition book. When he began to read what was written on the blue-lined pages, he could hardly believe his eyes.

"Now I start my diary of my personal plot to kill by pistol either Richard Nixon or George Wallace," the first sentence read. "I entend to shoot one or the other while he attends a champagne"—meaning campaign—"rally for the Wisconsin Presidential Preference Primary."

Griffin had discovered the missing first part of a diary Arthur Bremer started on the second of March 1972. It was a 148-page chronicle, replete with every misspelling imaginable, of the author's descent into his own lower mind.

Bremer buried it on April 3 just before leaving for Canada to shoot Nixon at a state visit in Ottawa. The second part, some 114 pages, was found in Bremer's car after the Wallace shooting. It was subsequently published under the title, *Diary of an Assassin*. The two parts of the diary reflect two distinct phases of Bremer's life at that time. The first is the planning part, thinking about how to kill Nixon or Wallace, preferably Nixon because it would make a bigger splash. It records his ruminations about his childhood, his rejection of a world that laughed at him, his frustrated love for Joan Pemrich, and his developing compulsion to kill.

It ended with Bremer at last finding his real place in the world, his true being. He was an assassin. No, that wasn't quite right. He coined the word "assassinator" because "assassin" was such a pedestrian term. He was an assassinator. Even though he couldn't spell either word, he found his identity as an assassin and this identity gave him strength, purpose, and, deadliest of all, persistence.

The second part of the diary, started the day after he buried the first, shows Bremer moving to put his plans into action. It depicts him on the move, stalking first Nixon and then Wallace, making one wrong move after another but never wavering in his intent.

In finding the first part, Griffin figured he had a valuable artifact. He notified the press and offered it for sale at $25,000. From his prison cell, Bremer filed a $500,000 lawsuit to prevent the sale. It failed and Griffin retained ownership. However, at that asking price, collectors didn't judge it all that valuable. Griffin eventually sold it to Dr. James Pittman, dean of the School of Medicine at the University of Alabama, Birmingham, for $5,350. The document is now in UAB's Lister Hill Library, available to psychologists and researchers.

The full Bremer diary, with its careless spelling and drawings as crude as his language, is Bremer's real voice, the one that no one else had ever heard. He opened up to a school notebook as a kind of last testament, fully expecting that when he shot Nixon he would be killed on the spot by the Secret Service or at least have to spend the rest of his days in prison. He would be famous and sales of the diary would make him rich, though he didn't give much thought to how he could spend his wealth dead or in jail.

Most important, one way or the other, he would at long last have actually *done* something, something big and significant, something no one else was willing to risk. One pull of the trigger and he would be in the history books, up there, feared, admired, in a way immortal. One twitch of his finger stood between the failure he was and the success he was driven to be.

"It's worth death or a long trial & life in prison, life outside ain't so hot," he wrote. "I want to do SOMETHING BOLD AND DRAMATIC, FORCEFULL & DYNAMIC. A STATEMENT of my manhood for the world to see."

Since this was Bremer's life statement, he tried to dress it up here and there with some sociopolitical diatribes. But these were so vacuous that even the author did not appear to take them very seriously and he didn't waste much time trying to develop them.

One of his better samples: "A nice yellow moon tonight. A beautiful earth. To bad it has to be covered with cities of concreat. People running thru breakfast, to work, hating work, rushed thru lunch, running home, idiot box. If we all got together maybe we could walk at a normal pace. Or just lay down & watch the moon."

Like the cackling villain in an old-fashioned melodrama, he frequently studded his text with largely written HA HA HAs. One can almost imagine him twirling a handlebar mustache.

And yet more winning qualities come through as well: a surprisingly winsome sense of humor, all out of whack with the subject matter; an almost childlike response to small kindnesses; and a perception that, at moments, Bremer was trying in some way to resist the decay of his own thoughts and feelings. "Yes," he confided to the notebook, "I do have problems in the head."

It was this small, weak recognition that something was wrong with himself, that he was sealed off from the normal life around him, that gives Bremer an almost tragic dimension. One psychiatrist was to remark that he felt Bremer was living inside a Plexiglas bubble, where he couldn't be reached.[39]

Having stated his purpose at the outset of the diary, Bremer slowly began to make his plans. The first step was to gather information that would help him penetrate the tight security around the candidates. "I have to be within spitting distance of Nixon before I can hit him (or anything else). . . . Got to think up something cute to shout out after I kill him, like Booth did."

Only a few years beyond Bremer's age, John Wilkes Booth, arguably the most successful American assassin, shouted "Sic Semper Tyrannus" (Thus Always Tyrants, or, more plainly, they all get what they deserve sooner or later) after shooting Abraham Lincoln.

During this planning period, Bremer began to write about his life ("Just call me a canoe, my mother likes to paddle me") and the degeneration of his attitudes: "I passed from a self-destruct attitude to a 'Why destroy myself, I'm innocent. People

I seek only friendship from Kill me every day. Why not kill them?' attitude . . . I've had so many plans & schemes & useless thoughts and wasted energy."

One of these plans involved becoming a writer and film reviewer. One of his favorite movies was *Klute*, starring Jane Fonda and Donald Sutherland, which he summarized this way: "A whore who doesn't know herself & can't feel love learns to love herself for being loved by a guy who she learns to love for being the one to love her. Gee, I write reviews just like the pros."

As his plans for death, Nixon's and his own, matured, Bremer began to suffer crises of confidence, which took the form of hypochondria.

> "As death comes close, I got nerves. Stomack. Pulse. Heart. Headacke. Tired. I must battel all this time for a few seconds chance at fame & suicide (or one hell of a shitty life waiting for trail, questioned, exposed, emprisoned . . . I need confidence, It will happen & be all over, very much over, in a few seconds.
>
> "I'm gonna, got to, kill somebody."

And in a reference to Nixon's campaign slogan,

> "NIXON'S THE ONE!
> "And how! HA! HA! HA!!"

But he hadn't forgotten about Wallace as a secondary objective. The governor, crisscrossing the country to gather support for the Democratic presidential nomination, was an accessible target. Bremer needed to test the governor's security and find out as much as he could about obstacles. As he observed, "It will allways be easier to get close to an underdog candidate or one who's party is not in the Honky House."

Bremer gained some valuable information at a rally attended by Wallace. To find out how close he could get to the candidate, he slowly moved to the front of the audience. "Noted how easy to get in and get close — about 30 feet. Didn't bring my gun or that would have been IT."

Reading the papers the next day, he discovered that Wallace routinely used a bulletproof podium whenever he appeared in public. He recorded a thought he read in a newspaper: The past is prologue. "Something to remember," he wrote.

Bremer recalled the disappointments of his short-lived college career, which he thought would make his life easy and rich. "I had thought 'colledge' (Yech, I can't even spell it) was a magical mystical place where I would 'learn' something important enought to give me an easy (thinking, not sweating) job & a fat salary (not wages). I found it only a poor imitation of high school (where I worked harder & was required to do more writtings) & wondered why I wasn't required to take college first & then high school."

But his dismal school experiences were only the most recent failures in a short lifetime of failure. Inside Bremer was a rage to succeed, to plan and take an action that would produce a result no one could ever ignore or laugh at. Killing somebody and dying dramatically in the process would be his definitive success, the preferred way to shake people awake and make them see that Bremer was important, that his life had meaning. "You see, ladies and gentelmen, I must succeed in something, if only my own suicide. I must have that or I can't go on living. (luff at that pun, go ahead you bankers & capitalists!) I am in the frame of mind that I want to hurt others."

As Bremer became more immersed in his plans, he began to turn his attention to his weapons, noting that he had to learn how to clean them properly. He also went to a target range to practice. The pistols frightened him. To his own surprise, the assassinator turned out to be a terrible marksman, barely able to nick a paper target. He realized he would have to work his way in close before firing. So he turned toward dum-dums, hollow-nosed bullets that open like umbrellas inside the victim's body. With dum-dums, accuracy would be less of a problem.

"Hurray!" he wrote.

"I've found I have some blunt-nosed .38 cartiges! These are 'man stoppers' (Killers, some Killers) tearing big rough holes into flesh. Rounded tips make small holes as they enter and have more penetrating power but for a 'kill' use blunt tips to really tear up and do damage. With that you don't need deep penetration to kill.

"About the .38—the stock sure is thin & small for my small hand. Not enought weight in it either. No wonder I can't kill a paper bull . . . ."

Shooting holes in paper targets made him think for a moment about his intended victims. Unexpectedly, he found he had to deal with feelings of conscience that momentarily broke through, along with fears of inadequacy and continued failure.

"The .38 scares me. It makes an awfully big bang, big flash, big recoil. Wonder about the damage it can do to a living, breathing man. Gunfire is not a quiet, harmless way to die.

"It's violent.

"I think today I learned that. It's ugly just to shoot at paper (of course, I had a certain man in mind all the time which may have activated my conscience).

"But to shoot at a man. One of you. A part of you. You. That's hard . . . . I can't hit any thing at a 50 foot target range. I remember firing over 100 bullets, 99 missed the paper, some of those hit the ceiling & downed plaster & dust, & one 10 ring hit. Still can't believe it. How does anybody hit with one of those things? No matter for me, I'll see the whites of his moler teeth before I shot. Then I'll be dead. (A very heavy trip, man. ((can't get no heavier.)) . . .

"But to plan, to p l a n. Ah, that's the bug. If my mind knows beforehand, it can build detours to perplex & delay my death-wish.

"And even my kill-wish. I have always been my own worse enemy. Today I am no different."

Later, he speaks about some of the feelings he could never express to others.

"No English or History text was ever as hard, no math final exam ever as difficult as waiting in a school lunch line alone, waiting to eat alone & afterward reading alone in the auditorium while hundreds huddeled & gossiped & roared, & laughed & stared at me, & planned for the week end & laughed & laughed."

Joan Pemrich, he wrote, was the only friend he ever had but he smothered her feelings.

"I was hungry for love that I demanded too much of her. While all my spare time was lonely time, her life was rich with family duties, respon-sibilities . . .

"Though willing to accept any compromise to retain her friendship, she would not listen to me, would not look at me, lost all interest in me, even though I shaved my head to catch her off guard (and show her that inside I felt as empty as my shaved head) stop her in her tracks just to talk. I thought we could always talk.

"I was just minutes away from suicide for days just before and for months after I found & lost her."

An avid newspaper reader, Bremer kept track of Nixon's travel schedule, looking for an opportunity to get close to his quarry while the president was away from the safety of the White House.

"There is to be an April 16 blast-off for the moon. This when Nixon will be in Ottawa, Canada. It was my chance again. Better arrive 1/2 week early to look things over and just in case he's early. Not really much time. A lot of work to be done. A lot plans yet to be made. Good bye, Mr. President.

"I have a date with history. But I can't hit a thing more than 10 feet away."

Then, one of his weak attempts at self-questioning:

"Am I all right and the world all wrong? (That defined as insanity by some) Well perhaps there are born these people who would of been better off never conceived. Who, if given the choice and all the knowledge they desired, would of refused life. 'No, thank-you mother nature. Not that family. Not that neighborhood. Not that country in that century. Thank you.'

"Read that psycopaths admit their crimes right away & don't try to hid their guilt. Publicity being a big trill to them. Other killers, 'more criminal than psycopathic', deny all guilt and do all things to cover it up & get their chief thrill out of this act they put on.

"Thought (for today?) Life was never meant to be permenent.

"Decided to use word 'assinators,'" he wrote in his final entry in this first diary, bobbling the spelling of his intended title, assassinator. "'Assissns' is so ordinary."

With his identity in place, it was time for the assassinator to begin.

◆

On April 4, the day after he buried his diary and started on the second part, Bremer took a plane to New York to investigate the feasibility of flying or driving from there to Ottawa for the Nixon visit. Fear of failure haunted him more and more, along with tortured sexual drives. It was as if time, as well as money and sanity, were running out. Everything was threatening to fly apart. The time when he had to kill was imminent.

But he seemed to be trying to defeat himself at the same time. He brought his guns along in a small carry-on bag and strolled off the plane without them. In the airport men's room he heard himself paged over a loudspeaker. One of the flight attendants found the bag and returned it to him. Unopened. With a smile.

He had $1,055 from savings and from the sale of his cameras. He stayed in a cheap motel in Queens and studied the Manhattan skyline through binoculars. He was appalled by the weeds and litter that choked vacant lots and the stripped cars that lay rusting over the sidewalks. He read pornographic books, watched late movies on TV, and "began to cry 8 distint times."

Scanning the nearby buildings with the binoculars, he saw a naked woman near a window talking with a fully dressed man. After a few minutes, she got up and walked over to him and they embraced passionately.

But did this really happen or was it just one of his heated fantasies, his own mind reflected into the wrecked landscape outside his window? Bremer wasn't sure.

He realized that attempting to smuggle his guns into the Canadian capital would be most unwise. Airport security and customs officers were too sharp-eyed. They checked luggage. Crossing the border in style in a rented car, more dependable than the Rambler Rebel, might be the way.

The diary was put aside temporarily and resumed on April 13, after "a life time of events" in New York. He hired a chauffeured Lincoln Continental limousine ("Nixon was in one today") and toured Chinatown, the Bowery, and the Wall Street district. Later he checked into the Waldorf but did not think much of the place. "They spend all their money on their lobby," he noted disdainfully. "The individual rooms are flops."

After three days, during which time he found he was too young to rent a car in New York State, Bremer decided to lose his virginity in a massage parlor. He assumed, wrongly, that they were all houses of prostitution. He checked the massage parlor ratings in *Screw* magazine and selected three or four he intended to patronize, one night after another.

But he couldn't go through with it. "I twisted my guts for hours sitting before the store with fear & anticipation" before giving up and going to bed. He had an eight o'clock flight back to Milwaukee the next morning but overslept and rescheduled it for four that afternoon.

That gave him time to have another go at the massage parlor. After pacing back and forth on the street, trying to work up his nerve and libido, he finally got himself up a flight of stairs and past the door. Since it was Sunday, there were only two girls there. One was a knockout, a blonde, leggy, Nordic girl who said she worked for Icelandic Airlines and did topless massages to earn money on the side.

"She led me into a room locked it, turned the lights out and lit incest all with her back generally toward me." He undressed and she took off her bra. She massaged his back. He then turned over, tumescent and ready for the real thing. He began caressing her. But full sex, she explained, was against the rules. She would masturbate him but that was all. Bremer was, in more ways than one, deflated. For the forty-eight dollars he had given her—the eighteen-dollar fee and thirty dollars extra for encouragement—he expected triple X-rated passion, something out of his pornographic books. He wanted to star with her in a heaving, groaning orgy, kissing, nibbling, embracing, twisting, writhing, climaxing to the heavens. But all she would offer was a helping hand. He told her that "she could push & pull on that thing for a week & I couldn't come."

Instead, they talked. In all innocence, not knowing that he was speaking the oldest cliché in the oldest profession, he asked what a girl like her was doing in a place like that. She retorted by asking what a man like him was doing in a place like that.

Then, all too soon, a buzzer went off. Time was up. He offered her money to come to his hotel room but she refused. Bremer left, the burden of his virginity heavier than ever. Another failure.

On the flight back to Milwaukee, he had a lot to think about: how to get his guns across the Canadian border.

◆

Bremer's trip to Ottawa was an exercise in frustration. In a near-panic that his weapons might be discovered in a border inspection, he nursed his ailing car from Milwaukee across Michigan to Port Huron. At one point, he realized that he had somehow reversed direction and was heading back to Wisconsin. He got himself pointed the right way again.

Stopping overnight in a motel, he accidentally fired the automatic into the floor while playing with it. Imagining that the noise would bring police crashing through his door, he quickly found a war movie on television and turned the sound up to the level of a real battle. In a few minutes, he forgot about the police and settled back to enjoy the show.

Closely examining the trunk of his car on the following morning, he found an indentation under a mat that made a perfect hiding place for the Undercover II revolver. To conceal the Browning automatic, he used a long-armed ice scraper to push it deep into an opening above the right wheel well. But he pushed too hard. The gun fell down between the well and frame, out of reach. He loaded Undercover II and, passing through a small town, stopped to throw the extra bullets down a sewer.

His worries about being searched at the border proved groundless. The customs guard waved him through with a few routine questions. Asked if he had anything to declare, Bremer was tempted to reply, "I declair its a nice day." But he thought better of it and assumed a mild, cooperative demeanor.

Once across the border, he revved the car up to ninety miles per hour, as if defying the police to catch him.

"Danger," he wrote, "gave me an erection."

He arrived in Ottawa on April 16, just before Nixon's state visit, and stalked the president through battalions of security police and phalanxes of war protesters. "Were the cops really afraid of these people?! Was Nixon afraid, really scared, of them? They're nothing. There the new establishmen."

On three occasions, Nixon's limousine went right past the waiting assassinator but he did not have time for a clear shot.

Then it was over. The few days in Ottawa had produced nothing. After Nixon's departure, Bremer began to slip into a primal rage.

> "My fire is about burnt. There's gonna be an explosion soon. I had it. I want something to happen. . . . ALL MY EFFORTS & NOTHING . . . Oh, man, I a werewolf now changed into a whild thing. . .
>
> "Traveling around like a hobo or some kind of comical character. I'm as important as the start of World War I. I just need a little opening & a second of time. Nothing has happened for so long. 3 months. The 1st person I held a conversation with in 3 months was a near naked girl rubbing my erect penis & she wouldn't let me put it thru her.
>
> "FAILURES."

Bremer returned to Milwaukee in a depression. "HA. Ha. Maybe I need a vacation!"
The pressure in his mind continued to build.

> "I had at least 2 night mares last night. Bad frieghtening dreams—that's a night mare aint it? almost never dream & now when I did it was terrible. Didn't want to remember them long enought to write them down. . . . Everything drags on . . . drags on . . . Don't think I have enought money to pay the rent on the 15th next month & eat that month too. I gotta get him. I'm tired, I'm pissed, I'm crasy. . . ."

At one point, his frustration exploded over one entire page of his diary:

F
  U
    C
      K!!!

Between April 24 and May 4, Bremer took a break from writing. "Needed some fresh air & exercise."

During this time, he gave up on Nixon. "I've decided Wallace will have the honor of—what would you call it? Like a novelist who knows not how his book will end—I have written this journal—what a shocking surprish that my inner character shall steal the climax & destroy the author & save the anti-hero from assasination!!

"I hope," he added, "that my death makes more sense than my life."

He again began feeling a general weakness and sharp pains in his stomach and heart. In the midst of inveighing against liberals and bad movies, Bremer suddenly diverted: "Funny . . . I've got nothing to say. Have I ever said anything?"

He went to the library and checked out Sirhan Sirhan's *R.F.K. Must Die!* and Shihab's *Sirhan.*

In early May he drove to Washington, D.C. His diary at this point is filled with frustration at having missed Nixon.

("Our great leader made an appearance in front of Wh. House to shake hands with tour-

ists the day after I left! . . . I could of killed him
for doing that alone.")

He also vented some tangled feelings about the
country as a whole.

> "You know, America doesnt have to be im-
> perialistic. She allready owns the free world
> by means of economics. Compare the G.N.A.
> of US with all of Europe. Japan sends what?
> 50% of its stuff over hear? America sneezes
> doesn't everyone say 'gonsunhdit'? Everyone
> in the leadership of Britain, Phillipines,
> Canada, all South & Central America & Viet
> Name lock stock & barrel."

But . . .

> "Most of what I write now is bleh. The main
> theme has left it.
> "Hey world! Come here! I wanna talk to
> ya! . . .
> "One of the reasons for this action is money
> & you the American (is there another culture
> in the free world?) public will pay me. The si-
> lent majority will be my benifactor in the big-
> gest hijack ever!
> "Yesterday I even considered McGovern as
> a target. If I go to prison as an assissin (solitery
> forever & guards in my cell, etc.) or get killed
> or suicided what difference to me? Ask me why
> I did it & I'd say 'I dont know', or 'nothing else

to do', or 'Why not?' or 'I have to kill somebody'. That's how far gone I am. . . . NURSE,
GET THE JACKET!

"One thing for sure, my diet is too soft.
Weakens my posture maybe affects my insides
too. I am one sick assissin. Pun! Pun! . . . Who
would think an assissin weak hearted?"

By May 13, Bremer was on his way east to hunt
Wallace in the Michigan primary. He bought a pa-
per and read that Wallace's next rally would be in
Dearborn that night at eight o'clock.

At the Dearborn Youth Center, the hall was
packed and he couldn't get in. He searched around
and found the stage door through which Wallace
would have to leave. There were windows nearby,
lined with people looking into the hall. Bremer got
a place near one of them. He could see Wallace inside giving his speech. "I was all set. Jacket opened.
A still cat before he springs. Waiting . . .
Waiting . . . He's left the podium!"

Just then, two teenage girls stepped between
Bremer and the window. He thought that if he shot
through the glass it would shatter and they would
be blinded and disfigured. "I let Wallace go only to
spare these 2 stupid innocent delighted kids. We
pounded on the window together at the governor."

The next day he read that Wallace would
appearthat night in Cadillac, in a school gym.
Bremer was there. He got a seat about thirty-five
feet from Wallace. When the speech ended, Bremer
yelled, "Shake hands! Shake hands!" pushing at

people in front of him to get through. But the crowd had been unresponsive, so Wallace ducked out. As with Nixon, his limousine drove right past the frustrated assassinator, who walked back to his own car "swearing, swearing, swearing."

Bremer followed the governor to the National Guard Armory in Kalamazoo, where Wallace was to speak at a twenty-five dollar a plate dinner before returning briefly to Montgomery and then going on to Maryland.

"I'll soon be on the front steps of the Kalamazoo Armory to welcome him," Bremer wrote in his final entry. "Is there anything else to say? My cry upon firing will be, 'A penny for your thoughts.'"

Bremer did not even get close to Wallace at Kalamazoo, although the police got close to him. He arrived early and parked in the rain across the street from the armory. A policeman approached the car and asked what he was doing there. Bremer said he was merely waiting for the rally to start, and the cop, who had no reason for further suspicions, left him alone.

Bremer spent the weekend gentling his failing automobile to Maryland, to the rallies at Wheaton and Laurel. Car, money, and mind were nearly depleted. His smile was frozen.

◆

Arthur Bremer went on trial May 30, 1972, in the county courthouse in Upper Marlboro, Maryland. He was charged with four counts of attempted murder, assault with intent to murder, assault and battery, and carrying and using a handgun. The victims were Wallace, Nick Zarvos, Dora Thompson, and Captain E.C. Dothard of the Alabama State Police, Wallace's bodyguard.

Circuit Court Judge Ralph W. Powers presided. The prosecutor was Arthur A. Marshall, Jr., state attorney for Prince George's County. He was assisted by Elias Silverstein, assistant state's attorney. Benjamin Lipsitz, Bremer's court-appointed lawyer, was assisted by his daughter, Eleanor. Bremer entered a plea of not guilty by reason of insanity.

Much of the trial was taken up with the evaluations of Bremer's capacity to appreciate what he was doing and conform to the law. As clinical psychologist James Eric Olsson, who administered a number of tests for the prosecution, testified, "A person may be quite mentally ill but his functioning—meaning being able to carry on his daily life—may not be that impaired."

Prosecution and defense psychologists climbed through Bremer's mind on ladders of standard physical and psychological tests as well as lengthy interviews. He was physically strong and healthy, despite his diet of fast foods. His "weak heart" and other ailments were pronounced to be symptoms of tension and imagination. The Bender-Gestalt test revealed no organic brain damage. He also did well on tests measuring his store of information, accuracy of perceptions, and knowledge of social situations. He did not do as well on investigations into his mathematical and organizational ability.

The test batteries included the Rorschach Ink Blot Test, a series of ten cards in which a person can imagine scenes, people, and objects; The Minnesota Multiphasic Personality Inventory, 566 questions designed to probe into different areas of the personality; the Thematic Apperception Test, which involves making up stories about neutral scenes and people; the Benton Visual Retention Test, another examination for brain damage; a sentence completion test, and the House-Tree-Person Test, in which the subject draws a house, a tree, a person, and, finally, someone of the opposite sex.

Bremer's handling of the Rorschach ink blots was one for the books. Most subjects who take the test give between 100 and 130 responses to the blots. Bremer, striving to do really well, chalked up more than eight hundred. He found objects in the most minute shapes, saw red blood where the ink was gray and perceived shattered glass, food stains on a floor, and a figure with a bullet hole in its head.

The tests results gave the clinical psychologists and psychiatrists a base of data about Bremer to augment their gut perceptions. Interviews also were held with Bremer's family, schoolteachers, employers, supervisors, and co-workers to gain information about the ways he reacted in different life situations.

In the meantime, the press published authoritative analyses by academicians and social scientists on the implications of Bremer's act, much of it based on outdated or simply wrong information. Sociologists and others, especially intellectuals influenced by sociological dogma, are ever on the prowl to find new evidence, and new symbols, of society's manifold failings. Bremer thus became the moment's darling of social dysfunction.

A prime example was a long meditation by an English professor who had read about Bremer's original IQ score of 92 and divined in it an undiscovered defect of society: nothing less than the nation's educational system. Its rigid emphasis on scholastic conformity and compulsory achievement, he wrote, occurring just when a new hormonal onslaught boils through adolescent bodies, puts unbearable pressure on those of low mentality and violent proclivities. In past agrarian times, someone of such limited intelligence and frustrated emotions might have been insulated from his deadly urges by family and community. He might even have been able to make a contribution by doing dull but useful work, perhaps as a farm laborer, that did not strain his meager intellectual inventory. But the world has changed and new approaches, presumably sociological, were needed.

The professor's lament was heartfelt but irrelevant. Bremer had to take the Wechsler Adult Intelligence Scale test and this time he scored 114, or high average intellectual endowment. Whatever society was doing to those of sparse brainpower, Bremer clearly was not one of them. However, that did not prevent him from serving as a useful symbol for social commentators as long as the media's attention span endured.

Bremer rather enjoyed all this notice.

"It's tough to be a star," he remarked to one of his interviewers. He cheerfully urged his visiting mother not to miss the trial.

The prosecution had an overwhelming case. Laurens Pierce's film of the shooting was shown to the jury. Other witnesses had seen Bremer do it. The concluding portion of Bremer's diary was read into the record. The revolver he had used was identified as the one he purchased from Casanova Guns. Detectives found the automatic in the car. A parade of psychiatrists testified that, in their judgment, Bremer knew what he was doing and could have conformed his behavior to the law. A countermarch of defense psychiatrists argued the opposite. So much came out about Bremer's life that he was reduced to convulsive sobbing.

Lipsitz fought like a tiger for his client. In contrast to Marshall's quiet style, Lipsitz displayed a range of emotions—anger, compassion, rightousness, humor—anything he could do to sway the jury. He entered so many objections and motions to strike testimony that he often exasperated Powers, even though the judge understood that Lipsitz was attempting to build a record for future appeal.

The trial moved swiftly under Powers's firm guidance. On August 4, the jury convicted Bremer on all counts. Asked if he had a statement to make, Bremer arose and said, "Well, Mr. Marshall mentioned that he would like society to be protected from someone like me. Looking back on my life, I would have liked it if society had protected me from myself."

Powers sentenced him to sixty-three years in state prison. The following month a three-judge panel met to review the sentence. Lipsitz made an emotional appeal for reduction.

"They call the system that administers the punishment of criminal defendants . . . the Department of Correctional Services," he stated, "not the Department of Prisons, the Bureau of Jails . . . And if the purpose is correction, if it truly is, how do you fit that in with a sentence like this? How is anybody in this circumstance, with this sort of sentence, going to be corrected? You start locking up men in cages for the duration of their lives and . . . I would be trying to go through the walls with my fingernails . . . . Where is the hope? Why should a man do anything except beat his head on a bar or in a corner? What is it going to get him? . . ."

He pleaded for the panel to give Bremer "at least a hope, a glimmer of light somewhere down this long tunnel, where this kid can see his way out of this thing, where this boy has some reason and some incentive to try to live, to try to change, to try to become something worthwhile in the world and not just a vegetable or a charge on the public sitting there and evaporating . . . ."

The judges reduced Bremer's sentence to fifty-three years.

◆

The question reasserts itself: Why? To say that Bremer was driven to become an assassin because of his shabby home life and mental and emotional deprivations seems shallow and incomplete. We may call him schizophrenic, but the term simply identifies a class of disorders. It does not enlighten us as to their real origins and meaning and why they find such fertile soil for development in certain individuals. There remains a sense of something more which the tests do not disclose.

Dr. Jonas R. Rappeport, chief medical officer for the Supreme Bench of Baltimore, suggested at the trial that mental disorders can begin even before the moment of conception, depending on genetic history and such topical factors as the intoxication level of one or both parents.

This is more in line with recent biological studies, which suggest that many mental and emotional disturbances originate in disarranged genes and hormonal imbalances. These studies do not deny the importance of environmental influences, but they do point to a physical basis for mental illness that is at least, and perhaps more, significant.[40]

Even so, there remains a feeling of incompleteness. The genetic makeup of Bremer's siblings, and the intoxication level, if any, of the parents at their conception, gave no greater promise than his. Except for brother Theodore, a normal man who made a useful life for himself, all the Bremer children had been in trouble with the law at one time or another. But no other became an assassin.

Relativistic psychology had its day with Arthur Bremer. Psychologists found that he was deprived, insecure, unstable, explosive and somewhere between extremely peculiar and mentally ill. Such findings were not unexpected. But the workups still uncovered nothing that could help psychologists predict any more accurately where future Bremers are lurking.

For the fact is that many people have a dash of Arthur Bremer in their makeup. He hides among us. Many grow up in circumstances even more violent and deprived than his. Many conceptions are marinated in alcohol or drugs, and involve a medley of mismatched genes. Many children are the butt of their schoolmates' jokes. Many travel inward to live on happier planets, imagining lovely things for themselves, things spun of dreams. Many are vengeful and wish their tormentors dead. Many have low capabilities and dim prospects. But whether they go on to live successful lives or just scrape through, what virtually all of them have in common is that they do not attempt to assassinate anybody.

What makes the difference? When does a person's psychology veer off at a tangent into a real need to be an assassin? Why does an urge to kill, which virtually everyone has experienced at some time or other, translate into action?

Perhaps what is created in a handful of individuals, for reasons we may never fathom, is an unalterable tendency toward evil.

Evil, the great English playwright George Bernard Shaw wrote in 1903, is "a state of being, lower than ordinary people, into which one goes and never comes back."

The idea of evil, long scorned as a sign of Victorian-era moralizing or New Age stardust, is presently making one of its periodic comebacks. The June 4, 1995, *New York Times Magazine* ran a cover story entitled "Evil's Back." The implication was not so much that evil has been away all this time as that it is now getting another fifteen minutes of fame as some kind of explanation of our baser behavior. Scholars are devoting serious pondering time to the question of angels and devils, good and evil, while the entertainment media merchandises it all along with its standard offerings of violence and butchery.

The scholarly contemplation of evil already appears to be running aground on the shoals of definition and research. What, after all, is evil? How can we agree on terms and conditions? How can we subject evil to the scientific method of experiment and objective analysis? Comparing contemporary criminal phenomena with ancient religious and philosophical writings may make an interesting bounce on an intellectual trampoline, but it cannot continue for long. New speculations are bound to arise as thinkers grope for ways to explain the unexplainable: the Adolph Hitlers, the Stalins, the Pol Pots, the Saddam Husseins—even the Menendez and Simpson murders, and countless other abominations. And the logicians always fall down the same well: the pride of intellect. They try to think it through, as though there were some kind of reasonable, logical explanation for a Hitler. Yet no one ever finds it. Despite heroic questioning and probing, our minds still look for enlightenment from relativistic social science, the belief that wrongdoing depends essentially on environment and influences imposed from outside, i.e., society.

Thus, "our society," not the individual, is today's stand-in for evil. Our Society—usually expressed with a deprecatory adjective in the middle, such as Sick, Racist, Chauvinist, or whatever rage is most popular at the moment—is held responsible for everything that goes wrong in our lives. To blame Our Society is to blame not ourselves but our institutions and social structures. This is a great solace. It absolves us of personal accountability for our behavior. It allows us to heap censure for the often unpleasant outcomes of our actions on what is essentially a mental, not a demonstrably realistic, construct. Institutions exist, but Our Society is an idea, and a rather vague one at that. Blaming it for anything leads to a dead end. Viewed practically, this amounts to blaming nothing at all.

There is, however, a price for such consolation. Once liberated from the entanglements and responsibilities of ethical judgments, we become ensnared in psychological and sociological theorizing. To find and develop these theories, and elaborate new ones as the old are disproved or become boring, we depend on social theorists, many of them university professors, editorial writers, and specialists who gather and analyze statistics.

What is called social science today—it used to be known as social studies—is based heavily on sophisticated statistical analysis. Social scientists research, compile, organize, and analyze mountains of the same basic data about our incomes, expenditures, choice of homes, voting patterns, jobs and professions, recreational activities, eating and exercise, religious affiliations, organizational memberships, volunteer commitments, and educational levels. This is prized information for determining certain behavioral trends, especially economic. Marketers, notably direct mail marketers, and product planners depend on such data to find prospects and sell products.

But social scientists attempt to use these statistics to delineate the subsets of modern society and prescribe solutions for the ills they see lurking in the dim light. Invariably, they splinter off into disagreements about which solutions will work and how to put them into effect. Their overall track record is not encouraging.

Even so, social theorists are impressive on television, where they make lively debaters, and persuasive in Op-Ed columns. They tend to begin sentences with "Society should . . . ." "Society should announce that it will no longer put up with" one or another kind of outrage. Or "Society should take steps immediately" to solve some problem that society presumably created in the first place. It's as though society were a person harkening to all this good advice and weighing what to do.

While Our Society mulls it over, social theorists stand at the forefront as explicators and predictors of our behavior. Their views on how to make our social machinery run in harmony with their current theories are valued by government, the media, and other organized institutions, including the judiciary, religious establishments, industry, and each other. The consequences of taking theories for reality, and looking at people more as social instruments than as individuals, are now observable everywhere throughout Our Society.

The problem is that current social theories seem ignorant of the fact that we are our own social structures. Each of us is all of society. Society is not some amorphous external thing for which we have no personal responsibility, but rather the complex and always changing interactions between each person's ideas, beliefs, attitudes, values, aspirations, and behavior. In short, every human being is "society" and, as such, the keeper of its substance and purpose.

If we accept, then, that evil originates in the individual rather than the unseeing social mass, we are led to a serious consideration of Shaw's definition of evil as a state of being, lower than all the levels that constitute the norms of humanity. Once in its grip, escape is impossible.

So we may take evil not as fanciful devils but as a level of life lower than all the levels in the incredibly vast scale of humanity. This is the dimension of the monsters, the Hitlers and Stalins. This dimension has magnetism and weight. It attracts something in us. If it were not for a dimension *above* the scale of humanity, represented to us by the Buddha, Moses and the great Jewish prophets, Mohammed, and Jesus Christ, there would be no hope for humanity. It is far easier to be carried down than lifted up.

So if evil is something morally and ethically reprehensible and degenerate, something sinful and corrupt in the extreme, something reaching from underneath into the immense variety of ordinary, normal life, then it can be seen in Bremer's diaries that he struggled all too weakly with some form of evil that existed in himself, and that this evil eventually took him over and turned this lonely, strange figure into an assassin. He lacked the inner resources to fight against forces, influences, and pressures that pulled him down further and further until he could no longer defend his own humanity and found himself at a dimension of life below that of a human being.

What is it that can pull susceptible people down to what we call evil, that lower level of being within themselves, from which few, if any, can ever escape?

One of the psychiatrists who examined Bremer may have provided a clue. Dr. Eugene B. Brody noted in his testimony Bremer's "lack of congruence between thoughts and feelings, this splitting between thinking and feeling" that caused him to see things "in purely intellectual terms."[41]

It was this split that denied Bremer the intelligence of integrated thought and feeling and thus the real inner perception that what he was planning was morally wrong and would actually hurt somebody. When Bremer wrote that "to shoot at a man. One of you. A part of you. You. That's hard," he had a grip, if only for a moment, on his common humanity with others. But the grasp was too weak and he quickly lost it.

Building on Shaw's insight, we can posit that evil works through whatever separates a person physically, emotionally, and intellectually, and therefore morally, and makes him less than human; whatever causes a man to lose his organization as a human being and degenerate to the level of a thing in a human body. Full human form but with, at best, partial human content.

Something always interposed itself between Bremer's understanding and his feelings, so that everyone in his life and thoughts—his mother the "bitch," Joan Pemrich, Sirhan Sirhan, Nixon, McGovern, George Wallace and himself—were not endowed with human qualities to him. They were totems, symbols, images, abstract ideas, some to be hunted by a man who had become something less than human himself, "a werewolf now changed into a whild thing."

Mark David Chapman, John Lennon's killer, expressed this clearly in a 1992 television interview. Asked how he would explain what he had done if he could speak to Yoko Ono, Lennon's widow, Chapman had a ready answer. "Please understand, Yoko, I wasn't killing a real person. I killed an image. I killed an album cover."[42]

In his diary, Bremer made a crude drawing of himself as a crazed monster and wrote, "Now I bare my fangs!"

◆

Bremer's boast that "I am as important as the start of World War I" brings a wider dimension to the question of lost humanity. The First World War remains alive in the consciousness of Europeans, but in the United States its image is for the most part confined to statues in parks, dedicated to unremembered heroes and covered with a patina of green mold and bird droppings. Along with the War of 1812 and the Spanish-American War, it is one of our haziest national memories.

Because the brotherhood of assassins is relatively small and its members often appear to keep track of one another's plans, blunders, failures, and successes, Bremer, as deficient a student as he was, nevertheless had learned that World War I was touched off in June 1914, by a fellow wild thing, a young Bosnian named Gavrilo Princip, who set out to avenge Bosnia's annexation by Austria-Hungary.[43]

After a series of almost slapstick blunders, not unlike Bremer's, he shot—also at extremely close range—the heir to the Austrian throne, Archduke Franz Ferdinand and his wife, Sophie, as they rode in a motorcade of open cars through the streets of Sarajevo, a city of what was formerly Yugoslavia and is now Bosnia-Herzegovina, the scene of more recent depredations.

The occasion was a gala state visit. Sarajevo was celebrating the Feast of Saint Vitus, a holiday dear to the hearts of Serbian nationalists because it symbolized victory over the Turks in one of the region's innumerable ancient wars.

Princip was one of seven jittery would-be murderers stalking the archduke. Most were teen-agers. All were seriously ill with tuberculosis.

The motorcade sailed past the first conspirator, who did nothing. The second tossed a bomb at Franz Ferdinand's car. It missed but slightly wounded Sophie, two attendants, and a dozen in the cheering crowd that lined the streets. Three other conspirators, paralyzed by fear, stood rooted to the spot as the royal automobile sped by, just as Bremer, in Ottawa, watched helplessly as Nixon's limousine swept past. Another managed to get himself hemmed in by crowds cheering the pair, and he too did nothing.

After excoriating his mortified hosts for failing to prevent the attack, Franz Ferdinand decided to go to the hospital to visit the others who had been wounded in the assassination attempt. But the lead car took a wrong turn. The driver realized his mistake, stopped, and began to turn around.

That action started a war that engulfed the hitherto civilized world.

Princip, the last of the plotters, was waiting less than five feet away. He didn't even have to aim. Drawing his pistol, he jumped on the car and put a single bullet into each of the royal occupants.

"Sophie, don't die!" cried the archduke. His wife was staring straight ahead. Then she fell over dead. A moment later, he collapsed beside her. It was their fourteenth wedding anniversary.[44]

Three years later, nearly forgotten in a prison cell as war decimated Europe, the tubercular Princip followed his victims.

Archduke Franz Ferdinand was hardly a preeminent world figure at the time, and few people were much concerned about his fate. Aside from adoring his wife, Franz Ferdinand had little to recommend him. He was as overbearing as any modern bureaucrat. But in Europe's convoluted politics of the day, with nations spoiling for a good fight, the double assassination led Austria-Hungary to declare war on Serbia, and from that small spark, the continent exploded. Within weeks, an ebullient Europe marched off with blind, romantic joy to the first great technological war, a meat-grinder that may still be unparalleled for its inhumanity.

Millions of young men, including the brightest of their generation, could hardly wait to get into the trenches. There they were transformed into wild things with fangs, tearing each other to pieces with the first machine guns, the first massive use of repeating rifles, the first fighting airplanes, the first flame throwers (initially used against massed troops and later against the first tanks), the first poison gas, the first long-range artillery, and the first fragmentation hand grenades, as well as the more traditional swords, knives, brass knuckles, clubs, boots, bare hands, and even teeth.

The sorrow came later. Ten million soldiers died in that unspeakable war and six million more were seriously wounded. Millions more civilians and refugees, the first on such a large scale, suffered immeasurable and, for the most part, unrecorded agony. At the end, famine and influenza raged through Germany. Without food or coal, families huddled together in their beds for warmth and the inevitable products of the rise in incest haunted that nation for years, perhaps rattling their chains through the immigrant family of Sylvia Imse Bremer.[45]

As with all wars, a number of soldiers who survived reported that they had lost their feelings for the enemy's humanity and had become cold, calculating minds or, conversely, boiling rages without thought.

Setting all this horror in motion was the gift, the poisoned apple, of Princip the assassin, to whose station Arthur Bremer aspired.

In the proper conditions, such as war, anybody can become an Arthur Bremer or much worse. The split between mind and feelings is one opening through which anyone can fall to the lower level of life where evil, no longer simply a quaint moralistic concept or field of study, in fact rules.

But Bremer himself did not need conditions. Poor, weak Artie, locked away in his uncomprehending mind, unable to resist, fell through that split all alone and became the wild thing, baring his teeth and striking, an assassin of George Wallace's national political ambitions, a giver of life-long pain.

Arthur Bremer had at least some recognition of the lower nature of his mind. But for the rest of us, splintered as we are by values debased to the level of bumper stickers, by our self-imposed slavery to pop sophistries of the day, and by the intemperate and punitive influences of public opinion molders, evil wanders freely through our lives, unrecognized and therefore denied. In that denial lies its over-whelming power.

◆

When Bremer was in the Baltimore County jail, he remarked to an interviewer: "This is the happiest home I ever had."

In May 1987, on the fifteenth anniversary of the shooting, an Associated Press story gave a brief look at Bremer's life in the federal prison at Hagerstown, Maryland. He still had his odd sense of humor. Asked by a prison teacher to catalogue books in the library, the AP reported, he added nonexistent titles such as "How to Catch Girls" and "How to Fix Cars," two of the problems least likely to vex him and his fellow inmates.

Bremer's privacy is respected. He has a cell to himself and keeps to himself. People still write to him but he does not reply. He does not give inter-views. Far from his original idea of selling his story for a fortune, he is now—publicly and officially—silent. He is at last able to control the world by shut-ting it out. He became eligible for parole in June 1985 but has refused to request a hearing. Without such a request, no action on parole can be initiated.

Apparently, the assassinator has found his way home.

III

Pain and Spirit

AS HE LAY ON THE BLACKTOP, WALLACE KNEW
he was paralyzed. "I can't move my legs," he
groaned to Cornelia. A Secret Service agent, William Breen, knelt beside Wallace and tried to take
his pulse. "Who are you?" the governor asked. Breen
identified himself. "Put your gun up," Wallace ordered. "I've been shot enough for one day." Breen
gasped. He hadn't realized he was still clutching
his service revolver.

While police and campaign workers tried to get
the crowd to move back, calls for a Rescue Squad
ambulance went out.

A seventy-six-year-old doctor, Bryan Warren,
pushed through the onlookers. Moments later he
was joined by a second physician, Frank C. Bruno.
A former flight surgeon in Vietnam, Bruno had
experience with paraplegics. The moment he saw
Wallace he thought "Paralysis."

The doctors opened Wallace's shirt. The bullet
hole in the chest was hardly bleeding. That was a
bad sign. It indicated a strong possibility that the
bleeding was internal. Fearful it might be a "suck-
ing" wound caused by a punctured lung, Bruno put

a handkerchief over the hole. To his relief, there was no pull on the cloth.

Suddenly, Wallace's breathing became labored. Bruno, fearful of losing Wallace right there, decided not to wait for the ambulance. He had the Secret Service men pick Wallace up and put him in a station wagon for transport to a nearby hospital. But as they were about to leave, the Laurel Rescue Squad ambulance raced up. Fortunately for Wallace, this first-rate volunteer unit held awards for speed and efficiency. Headquartered four blocks away, the ambulance arrived less than three minutes after the call went out.

Wallace and E. C. Dothard, his bodyguard, were lifted inside. Cornelia, campaign manager Billy Joe Camp, campaign aide Emmett Eaton, and two Rescue Squad members climbed in after them. Other attendants and Secret Service men leaped in front with the driver, James Mills.

The ambulance jumped forward. But the rear door was still open and the two stretchers began to slide out. Hands clutched for them while the passengers shouted for Mills to stop. He slammed to a halt. The stretchers were pushed roughly back, one of them hitting Cornelia painfully in a shin, and the door was secured. Then they were off again.

Mills first headed for Leland Memorial Hospital, where Nick Zarvos, the Secret Service agent, was taken for treatment of his throat wound. But Mills soon changed course for Holy Cross Hospital in Silver Spring, Maryland, a fifteen-mile ride. Holy Cross was better equipped for such emergencies.

Wallace was dead white by this time but still conscious. He fought an attendant's effort to put an oxygen mask over his mouth. Complaining that it was hot, he reached over and snapped a side window open. Cornelia continued to soothe him and even got him to take intermittent breaths of oxygen.

As the top-heavy vehicle swayed perilously through traffic, Wallace felt pain for the first time. It was excruciating. He begged to be knocked out. "I don't mind dying," he moaned as Cornelia tried to comfort him, "but don't make me suffer like this."

At Holy Cross, surgeon Joseph Schanno had just arrived to visit a patient when a voice over the loudspeaker summoned all doctors to the hospital's "Code Blue" emergency room, where Wallace was just arriving. One doctor, himself recovering from surgery, removed a catheter from his arm and reported with the others. He was quickly returned to bed.

A team of seven surgeons was put together on the spot by Dr. Edgar Berman, a retired physician from Baltimore. Schanno, a cardiovascular surgeon, became the lead doctor for the emergency operation.

Announcing that there wasn't enough air for his patient to breathe, Schanno threw everyone but his fellow surgeons out of the crowded examining room. The expelled included Cornelia and the Secret Service agents.

The doctors then examined Wallace. They took X-rays and checked vital signs and reflexes. Wallace was still awake and able to answer questions. The

X-rays showed the stomach injury and bullet in the spinal canal, but the extent of damage at that site could not be immediately ascertained. After discussion, the team determined that the stomach wound was by far the more life-threatening and required immediate surgery. The bullet in the spine would have to be attended to later.

Cornelia placed a telephone call to Dr. Clifton Meador, dean of the University of Alabama, Birmingham, Medical School, to arrange for Wallace's treatment as soon as he could be moved back to Alabama. She also asked that Dr. J. Garber Galbraith, the tall, spare director of the division of neurosurgery at UAB and a college classmate of Wallace's, fly immediately to Washington with Wallace family members and join Dr. Hamilton Hutchinson, Wallace's personal physician, as consultants for the medical team. Galbraith had removed a brain tumor from Wallace's mother a month earlier and become friendly with the Wallaces during their visits.[44]

When the doctors realized that Cornelia was standing outside the door, they brought her back to ask about Wallace's medical history. She told them he was allergic to sulfa. Schanno discussed their worries about the plate of food Wallace had for lunch. Those bits of meat in the stomach cavity were going to mean trouble.[45]

Meanwhile, it still was not known if the shooting was part of a conspiracy. So the Secret Service assigned agents to protect the other presidential candidates, Senators Humphrey, McGovern, Henry

Jackson, and Representative Shirley Chisholm. Senator Edmund Muskie was included in the list, even though he had officially ended his candidacy three weeks earlier. Secret Service agents also moved in to safeguard Senator Edward M. Kennedy and Representative Wilbur D. Mills, powerful chairman of the House Ways and Means Committee.

The hospital began filling with reporters and television crews, as shocked politicians arrived to be with the Wallaces. Maryland's Governor Marvin Mandel flew in by helicopter from the state capital in Annapolis. He met with Cornelia and asked if there was anything he could do for her. She requested the best doctors available in the state. Mandel promised to get them.

Minutes later she was back in conference with Schanno. He informed her that Wallace's blood pressure was dropping so fast that the medical team would have to operate immediately. She had no choice but to approve the decision.

As Wallace was prepped in the recovery room, Cornelia saw that Dora Thompson was also there for treatment of her compound leg fracture. When the two women pieced together the events at the Laurel shopping center, Cornelia had a disconcerting realization. If she had remained speaking with Dora at the rally, instead of following after Wallace, Cornelia might well have taken Dora's bullet. With her phlebitis, a leg wound would have been extremely serious, perhaps fatal.

A nurse came in to tell her that President Nixon was on the phone. Wallace said, "Honey, you'll have to go talk to the President." Nixon expressed his regrets and said he was sending his personal physician to be with her.[46]

The next anxious calls were from political wives who had undergone the same ordeal that Cornelia now faced. One was Ethel Kennedy, Robert's widow, and the other Nellie Connally, wife of former Texas Governor John Connally, who was wounded in the assassination of President Kennedy.

Cornelia stayed with Wallace until he was wheeled into surgery. After that, unable to sit still, she paced back and forth between the double green doors of the operating room and a nearby office. Meanwhile, calls from friends and family began to pour in and members of the Alabama congressional delegation arrived to express sympathy.

When they heard the news, Wallace's principal rivals for the Democratic nomination, Humphrey and McGovern, immediately suspended campaigning. Humphrey drove from Baltimore to offer comfort. McGovern was in Michigan but his wife, Eleanor, had remained in Washington and she went to see Cornelia that evening.

Throughout, Cornelia displayed what *The New York Times'* Nan Robertson called "courage, self-possession, and an instinct to protect her husband." She would not leave the corridor outside the operating room while the hours dragged on. A nurse periodically emerged to report on the operation's progress. After two hours the word was that the initial fears of damage to Wallace's liver were unfounded. He was holding his own.[47]

It wasn't long before one of the Secret Service guards inside the operating room banged through one of the doors and leaned against the wall, looking as if he were going to be sick. He had just seen Schanno pile Wallace's intestines on his chest as the doctor probed deeper into the damaged stomach area.

Family members arrived at the hospital. They included Wallace's four children by his first marriage to Lurleen: Mrs. Bobbie Jo Parsons, Peggy Sue, George Jr., and Lee; Cornelia's mother, Ruby Folsom Ellis Austin; her brother, Charles Ellis; her cousin, Rachael Lichenstein; and Jack Wallace, a brother of the governor and judge of the same circuit court from which Wallace had launched his political career. Galbraith had traveled with them on the state airplane and went immediately into the operating room.

While Wallace was on the table, Cornelia, accompanied by Camp, went to see Dothard in the outpatient clinic. The bodyguard was talking to two FBI agents. She was amazed at the change in him. His color had returned and he looked healthy. She guessed that the bullet probably had hit Wallace first and spent most of its force before grazing Dothard's stomach. Cornelia patted him on the shoulder and told him as much as she could about the operation.[48]

Wallace was in surgery for five hours. His hemorrhaging was brought under control. The wounds in his arms, stomach, and intestines were sewn up and as much of the food remnants as the doctors could reach were cleaned out. He was given eight pints of blood.

Then the surgeons injected dye into the spinal area to determine the position of the remaining bullet. After another consultation, they met with Cornelia and told her that Wallace was too weak for further surgery. He needed to regain some strength before the bullet in the spine was removed. They also told her there was a strong possibility of paralysis.

But, Schanno added, there was some good news. They found that Wallace had the cardiovascular system of a much younger man. This would help him stand the shock and give him a good chance of recovery. The governor, Schanno said, would probably never suffer a heart attack.

◆

The press, the Wallace campaign managers and the other candidates soon had a major problem. With the Maryland and Michigan primaries due to get underway within hours, they needed to know if Wallace was going to die, be permanently paralyzed, or recover his full capacities. Had he been knocked out of the 1972 campaign or, for that matter, permanently out of politics? What would be the impact on the primaries? Would there be a sympathy vote or would Wallace supporters turn to one of the other candidates? Of crucial importance: which one? And how could that shift be influenced?

The Wallace people put up a positive front but

they couldn't be sure themselves. Editors screamed for information about Wallace's condition. Hospital telephones rang all over the place. About three hundred reporters descended on Holy Cross, searching through the halls, interviewing anyone who would stand still, commandeering patients' telephones and generally tangling their feet in the hospital's established routine. Thomas Brandon, the hospital's public relations officer, finally had to set up a press facility at a boy's club a block away

Camp, anxious for a believable spokesman to reassure Wallace voters, asked Cornelia to meet with the media. She didn't like the idea. She had experience with reporters' harsh questioning and didn't want to cope with it all just then. But some of the politicians who were there encouraged her to go ahead. It might help Wallace in the primaries and they all knew he would need the energy that only winning can bestow. Late that night, a composed Cornelia went on national television without any script or rehearsal.

"My husband is in very good condition," she told millions of viewers.

"The children and I are going in to speak to him in a moment. Before he went into surgery he was conscious all the time and quite aware of everything that was happening to him. He was talking to me all the time in the hospital. I feel very optimistic about him. You know his nature. He didn't get the title of 'The Fighting Little Judge' for nothing. I'm very happy and I feel good that he is alive, that he has a sound heart and a sound brain, and all of his vital organs are solid. I can't thank God enough for that."

She didn't mention anything about the likelihood of paralysis.

In the meantime, some well-connected campaign staffers learned that the *Washington Post* planned to run an article saying the governor's spinal cord had been severed and that he was through in politics.

Galbraith recalled, "The *Post* claimed they had a reliable source. None of us believed that. There was no way anyone could accurately assess the spinal cord damage without going in to look. We hadn't been able to do that ourselves. Governor Wallace's people were extremely concerned with the effect the article could have on the primaries. They wanted the doctors to hold a news conference to deny it. I agreed to take part."[49]

The press conference was held just after midnight on primary day. As the head surgeon of the team, Schanno was selected by the other doctors to be spokesman. The choice proved to be a wise one. Schanno was a direct and gutsy man who enjoyed his moment in the spotlight. In fact, he and Wallace were so temperamentally similar that they later became good friends. Schanno refused to speculate about the possibility of permanent paralysis. The questioning turned nasty. Reporters assumed he was stonewalling.

Galbraith recalled that under questioning, "I just told them the governor was paralyzed at the moment but we couldn't say if it was going to be permanent. I was asked if the chances were greater or lesser than fifty percent. The fact that he had been paralyzed for more than twenty-four hours made the chance of full recovery extremely remote. So I said less than fifty percent. It was interesting to me that other major publications, such as *The New York Times* and *Newsweek*, called to check on the medical accuracy of their articles. The *Washington Post* didn't."

After the press conference broke up, Cornelia, Camp, and the campaign managers decided to have their personal photographer, David Cloud, photograph Wallace in the recovery room as soon as the primary results came in. She didn't tell him about the *Post* story.

The primaries were all Wallace. He soundly thumped Humphrey and McGovern, winning Maryland by nearly forty percent and Michigan by more than fifty percent. Massive support by crossover Republicans and independents gave him his first major primary victories. A survey by *The New York Times*/Daniel Yankelovich organization in Michigan revealed that Wallace's first win in a northern industrial state was the direct result of growing opposition to busing, higher taxes, and what was known as "the welfare mess." Only a handful of the surveyed voters said the shooting prompted them to switch to Wallace.[50]

Tellingly, the vote revealed that Humphrey, the traditional liberal, union-oriented politician, was losing his blue-collar constituency to McGovern and Wallace, who scored biggest with the workers. The

Alabamian won about half the blue-collar vote. This, added to his strong white-collar support, gave him the big win in Michigan.

His victory was less of a surprise in the border state of Maryland. That was Wallace country.

Cloud's picture was released to the press and made front pages all over the country. It showed Cornelia smiling at Wallace, who triumphantly held up the front page of the *Baltimore Sun*. The headline read: "Wallace wins in Maryland, Michigan; hospital takes him off the critical list."

Later in the day, Richard M. Nixon finally did what Bremer had been so desperate for him to do. He got out among the people. He walked from the Treasury building to the White House, shaking hands with passersby en route. His Secret Service men were grim. But Nixon made his point. He wanted to buck up the nation and demonstrate that public figures had nothing to fear from the people.

On the Friday after the shooting, Nixon rode the White House helicopter to Walter Reed Hospital, where he met Nick Zarvos, who had been transferred there. He then took his limousine to Holy Cross.

Wallace, freshly shaved and barbered, eagerly anticipated the visit. The attention he was getting demonstrated his stature. But it was also probable that Nixon and the others anticipated that this was Wallace's last hurrah on the national stage. Democrats could afford to embrace him—indeed, they needed to—because he was a figure of sympathy, with delegates for the Democratic candidates to divide and a significant following that would vote in November.

Cornelia Wallace reported that the two men exchanged some comically stilted pleasantries:

Wallace: "Mr. President, you're mighty kind to take the time to come see me."

Nixon: "You look as if you had a good night's sleep."

Wallace: "They don't let me sleep much. They have to turn me every two hours."

Nixon: "Governor, you look so well, you would think you were in here for a tonsillectomy."

Wallace: "These doctors and nurses are the best."

Nixon: "I can see they're taking excellent care of you but I want to extend once more the use of the Presidential Suite at Walter Reed Hospital. It's available for you if you care to use it. My staff will make the necessary arrangements should you decide to transfer there."

Wallace: "You're mighty kind, Mr. President, but if I get well enough to leave here, I'd like to go back to Alabama."

Nixon: "That's certainly understandable."

Nixon promised to send Alexander Haig, his deputy assistant for national affairs, to brief Wallace on the president's upcoming Moscow trip.

As he left, Cornelia remarked, "We expect to be out there running against you in November."

"I certainly wouldn't want to run against *you*," Nixon replied smoothly.

The parade of politicians continued after that. Lawrence O'Brien, chairman of the Democratic

Party, who had ignored Wallace in the past, welcomed him back into mainstream Democracy. Teddy Kennedy and Ethel Kennedy paid a visit, as did Shirley Chisholm. The black congresswoman was by far the warmest and most compassionate. She prayed over Wallace, and by the time she left they both had tears in their eyes.[51]

◆

Wallace wanted to return to Montgomery as soon as possible to have the spinal operation performed by Galbraith at UAB. There was a political reason for the urgency. According to Alabama law, if a governor is out of the state for twenty days, he loses his authority and the lieutenant governor takes over until he returns. Wallace and Lieutenant Governor Jere Beasley were not the closest of friends. Beasley would not present any problems, but Wallace bridled at the thought of not having power directly in his own hands.

However, the food particles that the surgeons couldn't reach intervened in the schedule. Abscesses, the first of many that were to plague Wallace, puffed out his stomach. There could be no operation to remove the bullet until they were drained and healed because of the danger of infecting the spinal fluid and, through it, the brain.

Wallace and his staff wanted to return to the University of Alabama medical center for the operation, mostly to keep Beasley at bay. But Cornelia intervened. "She didn't care about the politics,"

Galbraith recalled. "She was determined to do what was best for him."

So Wallace remained at Holy Cross while a new medical team was assembled. The spinal operation was performed on the eighteenth of June. Dr. Stacy Rollins, a neurosurgeon in Chevy Chase, Maryland, headed the team that included his associate, Guy Gargous, Galbraith, Schanno, and Hutchinson.

"We opened the covering around the spinal cord and took out the bullet," said Galbraith. "It was lying beside the spinal cord. But the damage was done. The severity of the contusion had physiologically crushed the spinal cord to the extent that there was no hope of recovery."[52]

Rollins, a heavyset, round-faced Alabamian who settled in the Washington area after medical school, had, like Galbraith, been a classmate of Wallace. They had their meals at the same dining hall but never got to know each other very well. "He was a short, muscular fellow, very gregarious," Rollins recalled. "Always surrounded by a crowd. Our interests were different so we didn't see much of each other."

The surgeons found some metallic fragments around the spinal cord. This suggested that the bullet had hit something besides soft tissue and may have caused one of the other wounds as well.

The two-hour operation presented no major problems. "You can't always predict whether a patient will recover from that sort of thing," Rollins said. "We knew the odds were long, but we were hopeful for him. It turned out that the odds were too long. Most don't recover from this sort of wound and he didn't either."[53]

Wallace also developed peritonitis, a potentially deadly inflammation of the abdominal lining. Heavy doses of antibiotics cleared it up.[54]

Shortly before this operation, Wallace came in second in the Oregon primary.

◆

Wallace and his aides determined that he would continue with as full a political schedule as possible and would go to the Democratic Convention in Miami in mid-July, even if he had to be there in a wheelchair.

In the meantime, he started physical therapy. First he learned the mechanics of getting into and out of his wheelchair. Then he began lifting weights to build arm, neck, and chest strength. He weighed about one hundred fifty pounds and would have to be able to lift his own weight. The ex-boxer was still strong. It didn't take him very long to reach that goal.

Next came the parallel bars that gymnasts use. He had to swing himself from one end to the other, a difficult task at first. He was fitted for leg braces and began to learn how to stand on them and walk with the aid of crutches.

At the end of the first week in July, Wallace was wheeled onto a government medical evacuation airplane. On the way from Andrews Air Force Base to the convention, the plane stopped in Montgomery so that Wallace, on state soil once again, could reclaim the powers of his office.

More than three thousand five hundred cheering people, most of them state employees, greeted the ailing governor as Dothard guided the wheelchair down the ramp.

After some initial shaky moments, Wallace launched into a twenty-minute political speech, his voice gaining power as he railed about the impact of taxes on poor people. The crowd loved it, and Wallace, who had begun suffering bouts of depression over his paralysis, felt the old surge of confidence and strength. Then Dothard pushed him back onto the plane and the delegation headed off to Miami.

Wallace's hotel suite was furnished with exercise equipment so he could continue his physical therapy. He was able to get around and participate in the pre-convention festivities. He and Cornelia went to receptions, took a boat cruise, and attended press conferences.

When he appeared at the convention, his legs in braces, and struggled to his feet to deliver his speech, the delegates gave him an emotional ovation. However, his hopes of influencing the platform that year were disappointed. The liberals had control, and the platform was the wrapping for their agenda.

Wallace entered the convention with four hundred delegates pledged to him. But this support did not go deep. His organization was stretched too thin to ensure that all his delegates were true-believing

Wallacites. In fact, many were crypto Humphrey and McGovern people, pledged to Wallace for just one vote or whatever the minimum legal requirements were in any given state. After that they were free to vote for their real favorites. So the applause was, to a large degree, for Wallace's ordeal, not his ideas.

Even so, Wallace had his impact. He had touched the raw issues of busing and taxes that would plague the Democrats during the fall campaign. The party did not see the handwriting on the wall that was so clear to Wallace.

George McGovern was the nominee. As the delegates cheered their selection, Wallace groused to Cornelia that McGovern had no chance. A candidate that liberal could never be elected. The prediction proved accurate. McGovern went down to such a crushing defeat at Nixon's hands that his national political career was over.

Just a little more than two years after McGovern's debacle, the Watergate scandal forced Nixon's resignation.

As the convention drew to a close, a new abscess developed in Wallace's abdomen. Depressed again and with frequent crying spells, he returned to the UAB Medical Center for another operation.

He recuperated at the Spain Rehabilitation Center in Birmingham, continuing his physical therapy for four hours a day. Wallace had to learn how to be independent. He painfully mastered the techniques of bathing and dressing himself, putting on his leg braces, and maneuvering his wheelchair.[55]

The regimen was interrupted by still another abscess later that summer, accompanied by Wallace's recurring depressions. These so alarmed Cornelia that she pulled strings to be allowed to sleep on a sofa in his room. This was strictly against hospital policy, but Cornelia didn't care. She felt she had to be with him and help him keep up his courage for the battle.

For someone as ambitious as Wallace, a strong, active man who liked to ride anything but a desk, who needed to be with people and in the center of things, the knowledge that he would have to spend the rest of his life in a wheelchair was devastating. Wallace's moods were full of despair and a certain amount of lassitude that hampered his progress in rehabilitation. However, he did persevere and made some advances, even if they came more slowly than his doctors hoped.

Gradually, Wallace began to pull out of his depression. The pleasures of politics always helped his outlook. With the aid of his braces, he stood to address a joint session of the state legislature. He began to make personal appearances and to get reacquainted with his desk. And he started to think about the 1976 convention.

During this period, Garber Galbraith visited him frequently and the two became close. On one occasion, after Wallace became more mobile, Galbraith invited Wallace to a medical society luncheon in Birmingham.

"He was still depressed," Galbraith recalled. "But he was the center of attention and he had maybe fifteen people at his table for an audience. I could see him start to brighten up."

Wallace carried on with story after story and was rewarded with a stream of appreciative laughter.

Finally, he told this one:

"I was campaigning in a small town. A farmer walked up to me and said, 'Governor, my grandfather is in the hospital. He sure would like to see you and shake your hand.' So I went to the hospital, met the old gentleman and shook his hand and told him, 'Well, your color is good, you look fine, and I hope you recover soon.'

"He and his family were grateful for my visit. But a while later I heard that he died right after.

"Later on in the campaign, a shopkeeper came up to me and said, 'Governor, my uncle is in a bad way in the hospital and it would do his spirits a world of good if you'd come see him.' So I did. We talked a while and I told him, 'Your color is good, you look fine, and I hope you recover soon.'

"They were all happy about my visit but I learned that this man also died a little later.

"Well, when I was in the hospital in Maryland, President Nixon came to pay his respects. He shook my hand and said, 'George, your color is good, you look fine, and I hope you recover soon.'

"Now I have to tell you, I'm really nervous."

"The table just exploded with laughter," recalled Galbraith. "The governor sat there grinning. It was the first spark of humor I'd seen since he was shot. That was the moment when I knew that no matter what else, his spirit was still intact."

IV

Dark Companions

GEORGE WALLACE USED TO SAY THAT HE always believed in biting the bullet, but now the bullet was biting him.

It was the shadow of the bullet that had been removed from alongside his spinal cord, and it bit with rat's teeth that constantly gnaw to stay sharp as needles. That shadow ate away at his spinal cord for nearly twenty-five years, chaining him to a wheelchair, consuming his health and vigor, sending electricity through his nervous system. The pain became a dark companion that not only would never go away, but that grew closer and more intimate with time.

The dark companion was at his side in 1974, when he won a third term as governor.

It kept him company when he again ran for president two years later. Wallace withdrew in the face of Jimmy Carter's primary victories. Wallace later told intimates that he had paved the way for a Southerner to be elected president. Carter neither confirms nor denies this publicly. But word in Alabama circles is that he is not very congenial to the notion that Wallace played his John the Baptist.

Pain witnessed Wallace's 1978 divorce from Cornelia, seven years to the day after they married. It looked over his shoulder three years later, when he repeated his vows with Lisa Taylor, a beautiful blonde singer who had performed with her sister at Wallace rallies. And it stood by at that divorce, too.

The dark companion was on the campaign trail when Wallace, out of office for four years, ran for an unprecedented fourth term as governor in 1982. This time, he courted black voters. He did something no one ever would have expected from the old segregationist. He asked black people to forgive him for his previous racist attitudes and actions. Appearing before the Southern Christian Leadership Conference's national meeting in Birmingham, Wallace admitted that his previous segregation stands had been wrong, though, he told the black leaders, necessary to win election in the Jim Crow climate of the early 1960s. He appeared unexpectedly at a black church and, in an emotional appeal, apologized and asked for forgiveness. The congregation prayed for him.

Was all this genuine or a cynical calculation to gain black votes? Opinions naturally differed, but it is notable that many in the Birmingham congregation wept at his remarks. Cynical or not, feelings were touched.

He won a third of the black vote in the 1982 primary and, because of that, went on to take the general election in November.

Why did blacks support their former nemesis?

Southern blacks know something about pain and forgiveness, and perhaps they accepted that Wallace really had changed and deserved absolution. They may also have figured that the devil they knew was preferable to the devil they didn't know.

In any event, in 1986, after a lackluster final term marked by increasing physical torment, Wallace retired altogether from politics. His last official act was to swear in George Wallace, Jr., as state treasurer. Young George, attracted to the national stage as his father was, ran for Congress in 1992. He was defeated.

Wallace's dark companion sat with him during a lengthy interview with Nelson Benton of Alabama Public Television on June 22, 1986. The segment formed the backbone of a two-part series on the governor's career aired in Alabama in the summer of 1988.

Aged, bent in his wheelchair, badly hard of hearing by then—he later became deaf—and speaking in a low voice, Wallace talked over his remarkable career and, depending on one's point of view, either clarified or reinvented it.

In the interview, Wallace described such incidents as his famous stand in the schoolhouse door at the University of Alabama—a piece of political theater worked out ahead of time with Attorney General Robert F. Kennedy to avoid violence—as "bad public relations . . . I'm sorry I did it that way."

The confrontation did, however, turn Wallace into a national figure. Later, Kennedy supposedly said that Wallace was the only winner of that alleged face-off. It made him a national figure and gave him the political stature he needed to launch his run for thepresidency.

Despite the fact that Wallace had deliberately established himself as the master segregationist of his day, he told Benton that "Our animosity here was not aimed against the black man," but rather against the federal government. Of his former racist posturing, he said simply, "That was a mistake."

So Wallace, approaching his final years and despite his overtures to the black community, sought to shrug off his one-time role as guru of racism, attributing it to mere miscalculations and a bad sense of PR. This is a hard sell to anyone who has studied his command of political public relations. It would have been more honest, and probably more accurate, if Wallace had just admitted to the wide audience what many Alabamians still believe: that he had sold out his own moderate racial instincts to get himself elected governor in 1962, but much more importantly, that he had truly changed over the years. It may be that the hellish companionship of his pain opened a deeper empathy for the physical and emotional pain of others, especially blacks.

But whatever the reasons, he did evolve from the politics of confrontation to the politics of accommodation. He never proved himself a friend to blacks, but by the end of his public life, he had at least gotten out of their way.

As J. L. Chestnut, a black attorney in Selma, put it in the Public Television series: "He grew up." And

Alabama grew up with him. At the end of the last segment, Benton asked Wallace what he would do differently if he could live his life over.

"I'm a human being," Wallace replied. "I err and make mistakes. But there's no use talking about the mistakes . . . . Just use them as education for the future. Not make the same mistake twice. But oh, yes, if I could live my life over, I'd live it a lot differently, realizing when I leave this earth, my life's eternal. And I realize now more than ever, as I get older, that nothing matters what you do on earth at the moment except what happens on the day you pass away. . . . Your spirit and your soul (are) everlasting and . . . conscious, and the most important thing to me has not happened yet. And that's the day of my mortal death."

Cornelia Wallace, watching the program, was unconvinced by Wallace's religiosity. "In seven years of marriage," she sniffed, "he never darkened the doors of a church, except when he married me."[56]

Watching the shooting scene with an aide, Wallace involuntarily clutched his side and bent over as if to protect himself. The body never forgets.

"Governor," Benton asked, "when you reach the pearly gates, what sort of reception do you hope for?"

"Well," said Wallace, "I don't want to talk about that, except to say that I expect to be there."

Two years after the interview, it was Benton who was dead of a heart attack on a trip to Washington. Wallace's fate was to live on, to endure physical deterioration, infections, and one medical procedure after another in a vain effort to make him more comfortable. But the bullet bit too hard, and the dark companion of pain remained steadfastly by his side.

There it will reside until the second death, the second assassination of George Wallace, is completed. The first death was the assassination of his national career, his potential to influence America's political agenda for years to come. His second death will come when the shadow of the bullet finally bites through. That death will move him from the news columns, television screens, and history books to his final resting place as a legend. Larger than life figures who die leaving the unanswerable question—Who Was He?—are the choicest candidates for legends.

In the meantime, Wallace manages to stay busy and, as always, visible. In May 1995, he rededicated the state Office Building, which houses the Alabama Medicaid Agency and Board of Pardons and Paroles, as the Lurleen B. Wallace Office Building. A small museum on the ground floor displays some memorabilia from both of Wallaces' gubernatorial terms. He also involves himself in the George and Lurleen Wallace Center for the Study of Southern Politics, sited in downtown Montgomery overlooking the Alabama River.

But, important as these activities are to him, they are peripheral to the larger concern of making his final peace with blacks.

Earlier, in March 1995, he appeared again with

the leaders of the Southern Christian Leadership Conference in Montgomery. He requested, and was granted, a few minutes to make a statement on the thirtieth anniversary of the civil rights march from Selma to Montgomery, which took place on March 7, 1965.

The original event was a bloody affair. Alabama state troopers, ordered by Wallace to disperse protesters led by Dr. Martin Luther King, Jr., did so with clubs and tear gas. That was during the era when Wallace made his famous stand in the schoolhouse door to prevent two black students from enrolling in the University of Alabama.

This time, a new band of marchers traced the route in peace, celebrating the men and women who had accepted to endure scorn and physical assault to march against segregation.

And again Wallace apologized, to the black leadership, to black people, and in front of the national media.

He sat in his wheelchair at St. Jude's school, unable to hear or speak audibly, as an aide read a short statement to two hundred mostly black marchers:

"My friends, I have been watching your progress this week as you retrace your footsteps of thirty years ago and cannot help but reflect on those days that remain so vivid in my memory. Those were different days and we all in our own ways were different people. We have all learned hard and important lessons in the thirty years that have passed between us since the days surrounding your first walk along Highway 80.

"Those days were filled with passionate convictions and a magnified sense of purpose that imposed a feeling on us all that events of the day were bigger than any one individual. Much has transpired since those days. A great deal has been lost and a great deal has been gained, and here we are.

"My message to you today is welcome to Montgomery.

"May your message be heard. May your lessons never be forgotten. May our history be always remembered."

Wallace joined hands with Rev. Joseph Lowery, national president of the SCLC, who helped organize the first march, and whispered to other black leaders who greeted him, "I love you."

Reporting on the celebration, *The New York Times* noted that reactions of the onlookers to Wallace's message were different. "Amen," said one woman. Others applauded.

But inevitably, some rejected this latest apology. Said one, "If he thinks this will ease his mind in some way, let him do it. I'm not interested in looking at his face. It brings back too many memories. Seeing him say that he's sorry ain't gonna do me no good at all. . . . He's trying to get right with his maker, that's what he's doing. . . . God's gonna make him pay."

But Rev. Lowery took a different view. He thanked Wallace "for coming out of your sickness to meet us. You are a different George Wallace today. We both serve a God who can make the desert bloom. We ask God's blessing on you."[57]

On whom? Is there a "different" George Wallace? Is there a real George Wallace? Is there a George Wallace at all?

"You want to know who the real George Wallace is?" laughed Ray Jenkins, retired editorial page editor of the *Baltimore Sun* and a liberal Southerner who covered Wallace's early years for the Montgomery newspapers. "You'll never find out. Because there isn't any George Wallace. Never has been. He's a fiction. He invents himself according to the needs of the moment."[58]

Politically, this is probably so. Wallace was certainly not the first, nor the last, public figure to be a self-created fiction. But editorial writers tend to view the world as a sink of political motivations. Surely there is something more to be understood about this strange, driven, charismatic man, a shaper of attitudes, an underrated constitutional scholar, a good ol' boy, a genius at campaigning but mediocre once in office, and a symbol.

Of what? Historians may yet spend many days of their years discovering that this question is not so easily answered. George Wallace has long been identified with America's race wars of the 1960s and 1970s. To many, he remains the arch redneck, the racist's racist, a small-minded, loud-mouthed, strutting little hate-monger, symbol of all that was wrong with the Old South. He was, after all, a major part of the upheavals of his day. The Birmingham riots, the notorious bombing that killed four little black girls attending Sunday school, the murders of three Northern men and a woman who went south to work for integration, and other violent eruptions, such as happened during the Selma march, were to a large extent the result of his racial muckraking.

But Wallace came at a time of change in the South and if he stood against it, as he did in the schoolhouse door, he did eventually get picked up and swept along with it, like most leaders who try to order the waves. It is not impossible that at some point historical attitudes could shift and soften. He could be regarded less as a symbol of die-hard segregation than of something larger: the ability to change, to grow, to admit publicly that you have done wrong and harmed people you never really wanted to harm, to apologize to a race of people and ask forgiveness. How many politicians have ever done this? How many could?

So Wallace, everybody's favorite symbol of racism, stands near the end of his life as a candidate for a different kind of symbolism, something more universal: a man asking to be forgiven.

This is an extraordinary metamorphosis for someone of Wallace's history and temperament. With all of its wars, officially sanctioned murders and persecutions, many based on the continuation of ancient hatreds never forgiven, the twentieth century has been called the century of crime. Yet where else than from George Wallace do we hear an errant public figure say, I have done wrong. Forgive me. And the spirit of this unforgiving age was summed up by the Selma marcher. No. I will not forgive. I want him to suffer more, because I have suffered. Forgiving George Wallace will do me no good. . . .

That is a common enough attitude. But as we shall consider, forgiving George Wallace could be precisely what would do that marcher good, much more good than he may imagine, because forgiveness is very much a part of people's lives. It has not at all been scorned to death in the world. As long as there is an instinct for civilized behavior, it never will be. Forgiveness is not proclaimed in headlines or talk shows.

But it happens.

The brothers, separated by more than a half-century of enmity and recriminations, never speak to one another. Years go by, and still they puff up their hatred as keenly in advancing age as ever they did in youth. Then one brother has a change of heart. He turns up unannounced at the other's door, drops to one knee and says, Forgive me. The other brother wants to throw him out. He thinks, No, Goddamn you! No fucking way! Never! But he can't. He knows in some way that by asking forgiveness, his brother has somehow *been* forgiven. Not by him. But somehow, in a way that he can't overlook or deny. He must recognize it. The weight of the world lifts off him. The brothers are reconciled.

A businessman gives way to stress and tells off his client, slamming down the phone on him. Minutes later, something happens in his mind. Something reverses. He knows that he must call the man back and make it right with him. Not because the other is a client. But for the sake of his own being.

He makes the call and says he was wrong. His relieved client replies, no, you were right. They too feel the lifting of a weight.

A man disappears, leaving his wife with five underage children. Twenty-five years later, he calls her. I am dying of cancer, he tells her. I have never been able to forget what I did to you. I am begging you to come and forgive me. She packs a bag and goes to give him the forgiveness he must have to die in peace.

Since Wallace has led us to the question of forgiveness, we must now ask what forgiveness is. There can never be an explanation, an analysis, a conclusion, and none will be offered. But we must ask anyway, so that we can open the question for our own sakes and perhaps keep it alive for ourselves as individuals. If we can do that, we may also find a new meaning for ourselves in Wallace's life.

Forgiveness is one of the deepest and most compelling questions that can be faced by any human being. It is also one of the most misunderstood, in that it is often taken for weakness and surrender when in fact it is the very opposite.

Forgiveness is incorruptible power. It is of a completely different magnitude than political power. Political power is the most evanescent, shifting, and, above all, temporary kind of possession. It's fun, to be sure, and can certainly be practiced with relative honesty if not pristine truthfulness. It inflates bank accounts—legally, in most cases, if not always honorably—as well as egos. In the eyes of susceptible young women, political power removes liver spots and restores hair. Those who possess it are great. Important. Everybody around them says so.

But political power fancies new lovers. He who has it and loses it can count himself lucky, given the temper of these vengeful times, to escape with his assets and reputation intact and his associates dissuaded from revealing his naughtier acts before a special prosecutor or on "60 Minutes." Still, the line of hopefuls seeking admittance to power's bedchamber is long and impatient. They will, of course, prove better lovers.

But forgiveness is real power. It wipes out a lifetime of hate and bitterness in a single moment. It restores a humanity that seemed lost forever. Because it is never possessed by anybody, it never betrays. It never changes into its opposite. It shows us truth unalterable by the pathologies of fad and fashion: sociology, pop psychology, deconstruction, feminism, masculinism, militancy, all the mental soap bubbles that float from the mouths of society-shapers and commentators, only to burst against one simple fact: To be human, we must forgive. And by extension, to be forgiven ourselves, we must forgive.

Forgiveness happens with a literal change of mind, an opening of the mind to a higher clarity. A person in need of forgiveness feels the weight of his burden of guilt. It is so great that he can no longer defend what he has become nor all the rationalizations that supported it. All that drops away, perhaps for only a moment. But a moment is all that's needed. Only with the new understanding this brings can he see what he is. This can mean the most painful anguish, suffering that drives him for forgiveness to those he has wronged. Only then does he have a chance.

This is repentance in its original meaning: transformation of the mind to a new level. A person repents not only what he has done but what he is. Penitence, a feeling of sorrow or regret, can of course be part of the experience of repentance. But the essential idea is that of a re-formed mind.[59]

When George Wallace pleads, Forgive me, some reply yes, you have asked and somehow been forgiven. Rev. Lowrey pronounced him changed, and prayed for him to a God who can "make the desert bloom." A man in need of forgiveness lives in a psychological desert of his own making; dry, gritty, inanimate, with no water to carry life or create a bloom of love. An unknown onlooker provided the Amen to Rev. Lowery's prayer. Rep. Shirley Chisholm didn't even need Wallace to ask. She prayed for this persecutor of her people from her heart, while others throughout the country either assumed a conspiracy of some kind or gloated and pronounced, with a full measure of righteousness, that they should have let the bastard bleed to death on the ground.

So forgiveness is not a matter of being excused for what we have done, or excusing others. It is a question of transforming our minds, of seeing ourselves in relation to the world from a higher point of view, and thereby rousing a conscience that accords with the higher principles of human life. We will, of course, continue to make mistakes and do wrong things, because we are not angels on greeting cards. It is our nature to fall short of our own aspirations. As long as this conscience is active in us, we will suffer acutely for our beings. But we will not fall to the level we call evil that so attracts our lower nature and that reached out and grabbed Arthur Bremer. Conscience sees.

Forgiveness, and everything involved with it, is thus a psychological process of a very high order. Any movement in that direction is cause for celebration.

None of this is a strictly religious matter, although religion is concerned with the elevation of man and comprehends the primary role of forgiveness. It has been noted more than once that forgiveness comes not from man but through man. It must be asked of man but can be granted only by some kind of power higher than man. Call it God, if you are of a religious bent, or, in Abraham Lincoln's memorable phrase, the better angels of our nature. Or, again, authentic conscience — something very different from social consciousness and the everyday exercise of blaming, criticizing, and excusing. Or don't call it anything at all. We need the humility to admit how little we really know. If forgiveness happens through us, let us acknowledge the fact and simply allow it to proceed without intellectualizing about it.

There is still so much we do not know and have not asked. The question of forgiveness is still not clear. Can't we just say we're sorry for all the bad things we've done and be forgiven? What makes all this such a big deal?

Forgiveness arises as the most urgent, most consuming need when a person understands in the depths of his mind and heart that he has done more than wrong; he has actually committed a sin. There is no intent to be biblical about this. The idea of sin comes from archery. In Greek, it meant missing the center of the target, the mark, the bull's-eye.

Psychologically, to sin is to miss the point of your whole life, to stand not on your own ground as a human being but on the ground of a false idea, a false conception of life that makes you something less than human. A false god, if you will. To operate from falseness, from an active unreality, is at best to risk living a useless life, one that will bring at the end the most heartbreaking questions: Is this all? Is this all my life amounted to? What did I miss? Why did I miss it? What was it all for? Even well-known, high achieving people have been devastated by such questions in the last hours of their lives. And at worst, living blindly and vehemently from false ideas can lead us to Shaw's lower state of being than the norms of humanity, making us unknowing agents of evil. Escape from this state is impossible unless something can quite literally make our minds new in the moment, so that we can perceive and understand in a new way.

When a person is brought, through whatever circumstances, to the sure realization that he has been the conduit for evil to enter his own life and the lives of others, that he has missed the mark and sinned against his nature and made others pay for it, then his awakened mind faces the choice of a lifetime. He can try to turn away from this realization, deny it, suppress it, and thereby twist his own psychology even more, making it still harder to escape. Or he can stand and try to bear seeing what he truly is. Then his mind can be transformed. For a few this process may happen on the spot. But for most it is the first step in a long and laborious process of building on this single moment of insight—sight within.

Seeing what he is in this way, understanding fully the consequences of what he has done, brings a person to his knees, the cry for forgiveness rising from his deepest being. And even the most ardent atheist may hear himself, in his despair, call on God. This is what is meant by a moment of Grace, and even though it is liberation from the tyranny of one's own psychological false gods, it is certainly not pleasant. What we may call Grace is emotional fire that burns away the lower connection with evil and lets us hear, for an unforgettable moment, the authoritative demand of something higher, the mark that we had missed all along, the central point that we had violated.

The person brought to his knees, literally or inwardly, is forgiven. This cannot be explained. It happens that way. No evil act can ever be forgiven. But the person who performs that act can be forgiven if his mind can acknowledge all of the consequences from the place of transformation and if he elects to endure the torment of the heart this inevitably produces. And when that person goes to those he has wronged and asks for forgiveness with all the sincerity of which he is capable, he does so, whether or not he is aware of it, as one forgiven. Still, for their own sake as well as his, they must be part of the process. If they have a sense of what the sinner has come to and is suffering, if something in them sees and is moved, they will forgive. Because they must. There is no choice. Forgiveness will come through them to the tormented sinner. It will use them through their unknown higher nature. It is as necessary for them to assent to this process as it is for the sinner to ask it. Forgiveness is equally for those who are sinned against as for those who sin. It is a priceless opportunity in a world that seems devoted to exalting grievances and intellectualizing hatreds. Besides, victims have victims. Everybody needs forgiveness. Some of us need mercy. How can we deny to others what we petition for ourselves?

But if the casualties of his actions refuse assent, if they force a choice, then their sin is equal to or greater than the one from whom they withhold forgiveness. It is a self-inflicted sin. They are left with only pride, anger, bitterness, hatred. These are the iron filings pulled by the magnetism of what is lower than common humanity. It pulls them in, and down. They have missed their own mark. They are lost and will remain lost until they realize that by withholding forgiveness they have created the need for it in themselves.

But here we come up against an irony that we must not overlook. Those who do not forgive are not to be blamed. They have their causes. The marcher who was not interested in looking at Wallace's face, who consoled himself with the thought that God will make Wallace pay, was still hurt by his memories. He could not see the price Wallace has been paying all along. The past still angered him. His experiences kept him bitter. We have no right to blame him.

Similarly, when Robert S. McNamara, defense secretary during Lyndon Johnson's reign and an architect of the Vietnam War, wrote in his memoirs that he had been wrong to support the war and had known it at the time, he touched off not forgiveness for his confession, but rage. And this is understandable. It is entirely human. For those who suffered in the war as combatants, and those who lost irreplaceable loved ones, such an admission comes too little and too late.

But while we cannot criticize the marcher or the war victims, we can feel intense regret that in holding these emotions close for so many years, in refusing to participate in the creative act of forgiveness, they are missing an opportunity for their own selves that does not come along often in the unbending world we have constructed. Those who carry this immense life question of forgiveness clearly understand that they cannot sit on high and act as judge, jury and executioner of anybody. They can only stand on the ground of their own experience, what they have lived through, and that is enough. They are responsible for what they know.

How does all this, incomplete as it necessarily is, apply to George Wallace? At the end of his life, he says he has changed. He asks for forgiveness. Can we believe him? Is he sincere?

Each person must decide for himself, and not all will agree. But in the end it is not important what we believe or disbelieve. We do not have to judge George Wallace's sincerity. His sincerity is really none of our business. It's his concern, not ours. It is a matter for his own conscience. It is enough that he appeals to all of us—those he injured and those he did not, and these can be the harshest judges of all—for forgiveness. Even if it's a ploy on his part to rewrite history and leave a more agreeable image, why should that matter to us? We are not demeaned by any impulse to forgive. And if he is sincere, if he has seen and suffered and been brought low, it is our obligation and privilege as human beings to say, if we can recognize the truth of it, you are forgiven.

So Wallace, ever the public man, ends his life in public atonement. If anything can make that life meaningful, it is this. Here at last is a real contribution from a one-time racist.

If we are disposed at all kindly toward Wallace, in view of his awful suffering, we can only hope that he will get his wish for something eternal— forgiveness—after he dies. His critics will eternally analyze, debate, argue, conclude, and reconstruct Wallace's life and actions. And new critics will come along to deconstruct the old. In so doing, they will build the legend. Will any of them remember the simple fact that there was a man there, intelligent, passionate, flawed, human? Who will find him?

And what of Arthur Herman Bremer, an even greater mystery? Like Gavrilo Princip, the primer that set the powder burning for World War I, Bremer had his moment on stage, played his part with devastating effect and drifted off into obscurity.

But that too is just the political side. Consider Bremer's unfailing response to human kindness, his unwillingness to shoot people on the bridge in Milwaukee after a waitress smiled warmly at him, his inability to risk harming two young girls who got in his way just when he might have carried out his plan, his struggling conscience, his need to have his own existence recognized so that he could be part of something in the world, even if that something was malignant.

There is a man there, too, approaching middle-age now, arguably in need of forgiveness himself, even though he has never asked Wallace for it. And who will find him?

Consider further what has come after Bremer: the whole march of the monstrous, uninformed by the most rudimentary kind of conscience, gaining media fame as symbols of one or another underfunded societal malfunction. "Human life ain't nothin'," said a contemporary killer on his arrest, glaring contemptuously at the news cameras. Death without thought or feeling, purpose or remorse. Evil without cause or end. These are the shadows on the light, the dark companions of our own lives. How will we find ourselves?

All we know about Arthur Bremer today is that he retains his interest in the news through periodicals and television as he lives out his life at the state prison in Hagerstown, Maryland. He keeps his silence. He is alone within himself. He does not speak of his own dark presences, the inner voices that tell and retell all the old tales of misery, pain, unnamable fears and isolation in the incomprehensible world that he has managed to shut out of his stone cage.

Notes

[1] Personal interview, Cornelia Wallace

[2] Personal interview, Cornelia Wallace

[3] *Birmingham News,* January 11, 1987

[4] *C'Nelia* by Cornelia Wallace. A.J. Holman Company, Division of J.B. Lippincott Company, Philadelphia and New York, 1976

[5] *Newsweek*, May 29, 1972

[6] Personal interview; *C'Nelia*

[7] *Maryland Medical Journal*, Baltimore, May 1976 A publication of the Medical and Chirurgical Faculty of the State of Maryland

[8] *Maryland Medical Journal*

[9] *C'Nelia*

[10] *C'Nelia*

[11] *Newsweek*, May 29, 1972

[12] Bremer Trial Transcript V, May-September 1972

[13] *C'Nelia*

[14] *C'Nelia*

[15] *C'Nelia*

[16] *Newsweek*, May 29, 1972

[17] *Maryland Medical Journal*

[18] *Maryland Medical Journal*

[19] *C'Nelia*

[20] *Maryland Medical Journal*

[21] *C'Nelia; Maryland Medical Journal*

[22] *Maryland Medical Journal*

[23] *Maryland Medical Journal*

[24] Personal interviews with Cornelia Wallace and Chief Archie Cook of Laurel, MD, police

[25] Personal interview, Lawden Yates, Alabama Forensic Labs

[26] Personal interview, Lawden Yates. Additional material from phone interview with Paul Eschrich of Sporting Arms and Ammunition Manufacturers Institute, Stamford, CT

[27] Lawden Yates; Paul Eschrich

[28] *Maryland Medical Journal; New York Times*, May 17, 1972

[29] All material relating to Wallace's wounds are from *C'Nelia* and personal interviews with Dr. J. Garber Galbraith, June 10, 1988, and Dr. Stacy Rollins, June 16, 1988

[30] Bremer trial transcript. Includes both parts of the Bremer diary

[31] Bremer trial transcript

[32] Bremer trial transcript. Also, *Newsweek*, May 29, 1972, and *Maryland State Medical Journal*, May 1976

[33] Trial testimony and *Maryland State Medical Journal*, March 1978

[34] Bremer trial transcript

[35] *Newsweek*, May 29, 1972

[36]Interview, Lawden Yates

[37]Trial testimony

[38]*Montgomery Advertiser/Journal* June 16, 1985

[39]Trial testimony

[40]*Brain Sex*, by Anne Moir, Ph.D. and David Jessel. A Laurel Trade Paperback published by Dell Publishing, Division of Bantam Doubleday Dell Publishing Group, Inc., 666 Fifth Avenue, New York, New York 10103, reprinted by arrangement with Carol Publishing, New York, New York

[41]Bremer Trial Transcript VII

[42]*Newsweek*, December 14, 1992

[43]*Wall Street Journal*, editorial page, letter from Peter W. Becker, Chairman, Department of History, University of South Carolina, July 16, 1991. Also *Newsweek*, July 8, 1991

[44]American Heritage *History of World War I*, by S.L.A. Marshall. American Heritage Publishing Co., distributed by Simon and Schuster, Inc., 1964

[45]*1918 - The Last Act,* by Barrie Pitt, Ballantine Books Inc., 101 Fifth Avenue, New York, New York 10003, 1963

[46]*The New York Times*, May 17, 1972, and personal interviews with Cornelia Wallace and Dr. J. Garber Galbraith

[47]*C'Nelia*; personal interview, Dr. Galbraith

[48]*C'Nelia*

[49]Personal interview

[50]*The New York Times*, May 18, 1972

[51]*The New York Times*, May 17, 1972; *C'Nelia*

[52]Personal interview, Dr. Galbraith

[53]Personal interview, Dr. Rollins

[54]Personal interview, Dr. Rollins and *Newsweek*, August 8, 1972

[55]Personal interview, Dr. Rollins and *Newsweek*, August 8, 1972

[56]Personal interview

[57]The New York Times, March 11, 1995

[58]Personal interview, Summer 1988

[59]For the groundwork of the ideas of sin and repentance, the author is indebted to the lifelong work of Dr. Maurice Nicoll, particularly *The Mark*, published in London by Vincent Stuart and John M. Watkins Ltd., 1970. Dr. Nicoll wrote extensively on The New Testament and the ideas of Gurdjieff and Ouspensky. Even those who are not interested in Christianity, Gurdjieff, or Ouspensky will find a rich source of psychological understanding in Dr. Nicoll's books.

Index

About Thomas S. Healey

An experienced speechwriter, editor, and writer of videos, corporate and consumer magazine articles, advertisements, and direct mail, Thomas S. Healey has specialized in international business issues for Fortune 500 chief executives. He holds writing awards from the International Association of Business Communicators and has been recognized as one of New Jersey's outstanding poets. He has been quoted in *The Wall Street Journal* as a top corporate speechwriter. A former newspaper reporter, he was an editor and senior speechwriter at Exxon and Texaco before turning independent in 1985. With the publication of *The Two Deaths of George Wallace*, Healey is now experimenting with new forms of psychological investigation.

A New Jersey native, Healey takes advanced jazz dance classes in New York City in the Mattox/ Pietri style.